Counseling Psychology
and Guidance

Counseling Psychology and Guidance

AN OVERVIEW IN OUTLINE

By

JEROME A. KROTH, Ph.D.

Assistant Professor of Counseling Psychology
Ball State University
Muncie, Indiana

CHARLES C THOMAS • PUBLISHER
Springfield • Illinois • U.S.A.

Published and Distributed Throughout the World by
CHARLES C THOMAS • PUBLISHER
Bannerstone House
301–327 East Lawrence Avenue, Springfield, Illinois, U.S.A.

© *1973, by* CHARLES C THOMAS • PUBLISHER

ISBN 0–398–02726–9

Library of Congress Catalog Card Number: 72–88469

Printed in the United States of America

BB-14

To Anya

PREFACE

Most counselor preparation programs are focused at the Master's level and take between one and a half to two years to complete. In that time the student is involved in two types of processes, a didactic or academic activity, and an experiential one.

The academic component of his program typically provides him with a series of courses covering the broad area of counseling psychology and guidance. These may include an introductory course in counseling and guidance or pupil personnel services as well as courses in theories and techniques of counseling, group processes, tests and measurements, occupational psychology and information processes, and a psychology core made up of some combination of personality theory, psychopathology, the psychology of learning, child development and/or social psychology. Finally he will likely take one or more counseling practica, a field experience where he is engaged in a series of counseling relationships with clients under the supervision of a professional counselor educator.

Counselor training programs, however, are very much committed to graduating effective, facilitative counselors and have long since recognized that no combination of course offerings will guarantee them that product. What makes an effective counselor is itself an illusive question, but general response to this need by graduate training institutions has been to provide students with opportunities for their own emotional growth and development. The assumption here is that for a person to help others he must be in tune with his own inner world of experience, and that this "tuning in" process cannot be taught in any three credit-hour sequence.

Increasingly students are urged (and are avidly demanding) more experiential activities for their own development, apart from their practicum. In the course of a Master's program a student is likely to go through his own individual counseling, to participate in a number of encounter groups, sensitivity training activities, psychodrama or marathon groups. It is felt that in these activities *real* behavior change and psychological growth can occur. Any of these forms of interpersonal contact can be moving and powerful events in a student's life.

The academic and experiential components of the Master's program do not always compliment each other. On the one hand, the student has certain courses he must take to complete his program (and which teach him some things that he needs to know), and on the other hand, he knows he only has so much time in the program, and he wants to experience as many people and as many other types of encounters as he can. Furthermore, he wants to increasingly engage in his own self-motivated individualized learning experiences apart from the traditional course sequences.

The purpose of this text is largely rooted in this conflict. A need exists to somehow telescope the academic portion of the Master's program to allow students greater latitude in growing in their own ways and in finding those kinds of activities they want to get involved in outside of the lecture hall. The book represents, I think, essentials of most courses students will meet in their program. It is, of course, very basic and introductory, eliminating most citations, most research investigations, most background, and in many cases some important details which belong to more advanced investigation. What it offers, however, is a condensed version of basic principles, facts, terms, and things one should know. It is an outline of introductory and advanced texts synthesized and condensed to present only the meat of counseling psychology and guidance. It is hoped this overview-outline concept will serve to accompany a Master's student from his introductory course, where it will serve him by clarifying and delineating basic concepts, through to his Master's comprehensive examinations, where it will serve as an organizing and review device.

In sum, the aim of this book is neither to replace other books nor to minimize the importance of studying counseling theories, vocational development theory or psychopathology more thoroughly. It is hoped, however, that it will speed things up for the student somewhere along the way so that he can devote more time to other experiences he ought to be having.

I would like to express my gratitude to Mrs. Pat Romeo for her help in editing and typing the manuscript and to Anya Stelle for the inspiration she has provided during the course of this project.

J.A.K.

INTRODUCTION

What makes a person real is his behavior, what he does, not what he says he does, or what his official title is or, what someone else says he "ought to be." He is what he does.

A person does what he does for a number of reasons. He was trained to do it; he feels like doing it; he was told to do it; he can't do it so he keeps on trying; he believes in doing it; he doesn't know why he does it. These are all reasons for why he does it. There are also a number of reasons why he doesn't do other things. Rather than introduce this text with an official declaration of what school counselors do and ought to do, and for what reasons they do it differently than counseling psychologists or guidance specialists, it is more important to say what is done and not done. In that way the breadth of behavior is shown, the extremes, the scope of activity, whether that be for better or for worse, official or unofficial.

The following is a sample of things which are done by people who in one way or another are connected with counseling psychology and guidance.

There are counseling psychologists who work in a hospital setting who do a kind of occupational counseling with sometimes quite severely disturbed psychiatric outpatients. There are other counselors who deal only with so-called "normal" clients who have some kinds of superficial adjustment difficulties.

There are counselors in schools who deal exclusively with emotional conflicts in children; there are other counselors who engage only in occupational or career counseling, steering away from any heavy emotional encounters. There are other counselors in schools who do no counseling at all, but administer tests and administer discipline.

Some counselors work with the unemployed to help them deal with the fears and hostilities of being in a job which they can't do without, but which humiliates them. Other counselors work for management doing staff sensitivity training to improve communication, effectiveness and industrial productivity.

Some counselors are in private practice; most work in schools and universities. Some counselors are teachers and some teachers are counselors.

There are counselors who spend their time sitting across a desk in a one-to-one relationship with a child; other counselors feel it is better to do encounter groups with teachers and to reach that child indirectly through the altered behavior of his teacher.

Some counselors take responsibility for maintaining the attendance and record keeping functions in a school. Some counselors are truant officers. Some counselors refuse.

There are counselors who attempt to read the pulse of the school, to maintain a "grapevine" spy network in order to anticipate and prevent racial outbursts or drug trafficking by reporting these events to the school administration or to the police. Other counselors deal with heroin-addicted high school youth in an atmosphere of complete confidentiality and secrecy.

There are counselors who tell a girl's parents that she is pregnant against her expressed desire. There are other counselors who know that their clients are going to have an abortion this weekend without their parents' knowledge.

There are counselors who act to mobilize social and political forces for change in the school and in the community. There are other counselors who fight to prevent change of that nature. There is a third group of counselors who feel that involvement in local sociopolitical realities is irrelevant to their mission.

Some counselors use sophisticated psychological tests to assess the relative effectiveness of using an auditory versus a visual approach to teaching reading to a child who cannot read, who is failing, and who is showing a number of emotional signs of that failure. Here the counselor sees himself as an educational diagnostician, a consultant to the reading teacher, and only lastly a person who is committed to maintaining a supportive emotional relationship with the child. Other counselors feel that the emotional relationship is paramount and that psychological tests are manipulative devices aimed at making 50 percent of the children feel that they are *better than* and 50 percent of the children *poorer than* each other. These counselors may do no psychological testing at all, feeling also, that a "test" is an evaluative device placing the counselor in the role of teacher, or judge, or expert, when, in fact, the counselor seeks to establish mutuality with his client and break down the barriers of authority and role which separate them and prevent them from establishing meaningful rapport.

Some counselors know little about psychological tests and use them improperly. Other counselors know much about psychological tests and choose not to use them at all.

There are counselors who see themselves as having a duty to support the standards of morality given in the culture through history. Other counselors refuse to serve as exponents of any given moral point of view.

There are counselors who swear with their clients. There are other counselors who will not allow their clients to swear.

Some counselors do research and believe the only answer to a question or a point of disagreement is through scientific inquiry. Other counselors derive their approaches from philosophy and religion and find experimentalism of this sort dictatorial or dehumanizing.

Some counselors establish token classrooms and train teachers to do behavioral therapy with particular children or with an entire classroom. Other counselors object to behavioral therapy on ethical grounds. Still others know very little about either.

There are counselors who find jobs for potential school dropouts. Some do local community job surveys and maintain close working relationships with city government to provide students with a wide range of employment and on-the-job training opportunities. Some counselors maintain a placement office in the school. Other counselors help students understand their aptitude and interest profiles to make an intelligent decision about their college majors. Some counselors are talent scouts for the Army.

Some counselors have experienced psychotherapy or their own counseling and have gone nowhere. Others haven't had any counseling encounter at all but happen to be effective with clients. Still other counselors have had moving experiences in a counseling relationship and are continually growing, becoming and changing as a result of it.

In sum, the foregoing is not a comprehensive guide to what people in counseling psychology and guidance *do,* nor is it an objective or unbiased sampling of what they do. Instead it is an introduction. Many people do many different things under the banner of counseling psychology and guidance. There is controversy. What was correct procedure yesterday is incorrect today. What was ethically sound in 1960 may be malpractice today.

The tremendous variety of behavior which exists in this field is in no way a call to forget the issues and to be comfortable doing your own thing. It is the opposite of that. Cognizant of the fact that this discipline is constantly reacting to the vicissitudes of new information, new practices, and new inputs, it is important to find the structure which embodies the change, to uncover the basic elemental things, the first principles.

There are basic things one must know to participate in the vitality and controversy in this field.

Counseling psychology is open-ended, changing, sometimes confusing. It is almost always interesting. To appreciate and enjoy its ambiguity and tenuousness, one must first memorize its vocabularly, learn its grammar and examine its syntax.

CONTENTS

Preface vii
Introduction xi

Chapter   PART I: PSYCHOLOGICAL FOUNDATIONS   *Page*

1. PSYCHOPATHOLOGY 5

    Normalcy
    Incidence of Abnormal Behavior
    Transient Situational Disorders
    Psychoneuroses
    Psychosomatic disorders
    Psychoses: functional and organic
    Personality and character disorders
    Acute and chronic brain disorders

2. PERSONALITY THEORY 24

    Sigmund Freud: psychoanalysis
    Carl Jung: analytic psychology
    Alfred Adler: individual psychology
    Erik Erikson: identity and the eight ages of Man
    Carl Rogers: perceptual-phenomenological theory of personality

3. THE PSYCHOLOGY OF LEARNING 42

    Definition of learning
    Classical conditioning
    Instrumental and operant conditioning
    Reinforcement
    Learning theory: contiguity, gestalt, purposive and S-R models

PART II: THE GUIDANCE FUNCTION

4. THE NATURE OF GUIDANCE 55

    Definition of guidance

Purposes of guidance
Needs for guidance
Guidance and pupil personnel services
Basic principles of guidance

5. HISTORICAL DEVELOPMENT OF GUIDANCE 60

Major historical trends
Important events in guidance chronology
Government support of guidance
Personalities influencing guidance development
Contemporary professionalization of counseling psychology
and guidance: APA and APGA

6. PHILOSOPHY AND THEORY OF GUIDANCE 70

Dimensions of philosophy
Systems of philosophy
Philosophy and guidance
Models of guidance: directive, eclectic, clinical, adjustive,
reconstructive

7. GUIDANCE RELATIONSHIPS 78

Guidance and the teacher
Guidance and the curriculum
Administration and the community
Guidance and the student

8. ORGANIZATION AND ADMINISTRATION OF GUIDANCE 82

Traditional organizational patterns
Other organizational concepts
Centralization vs. decentralization of guidance
Roles and responsibilities in the organizational scheme

9. THE INFORMATION SERVICE 89

Purposes and objectives of the information service
Types of information
Educational, Occupational and Social materials
Selection and evaluation of information
Contents of the information service library
Using information
A taxonomy of the educational scene
A taxonomy of the world of work

10. VOCATIONAL   PLANNING,   PLACEMENT   AND   FOLLOW-UP
SERVICES 102

The need
Placement
Follow-up

11. RESEARCH AND EVALUATION IN COUNSELING AND GUIDANCE .. 106

Evaluation approaches
Evaluative criteria
Outcome research in counseling
Experimental design problems

PART III: THE COUNSELING FUNCTION

12. THE SCHOOL COUNSELOR 113

Need for counselors
Certification and preparation of counselors
Counselor function and role
Legal and ethical bases for counseling

13. COUNSELING I: SYSTEMS AND THEORIES 120

Definition of counseling
Counseling vs. psychotherapy
E.G. Williamson's directive model
Frederick Thorne: eclectic approach
Albert Ellis: rational emotive therapy
Andrew Salter: conditioned reflex therapy
Joseph Wolpe: behavior therapy
E.S. Bordin: psychological counseling
Franz Alexander: psychoanalytic therapy
Carl Rogers: client-centered therapy
Victor Frankl: logotherapy

14. COUNSELING II: PROCESS AND TECHNIQUES 139

Factors affecting counseling
Counseling techniques
Structuring
Leads
Silence, reflection, role-playing
Stages of counseling
Resistance and Transference

15. GROUP COUNSELING 150

Purposes of groups
Terminology
Types of groups
Psychodrama
Marathon groups
Group content and process
Special techniques
Group counseling

16. APPRAISAL I: TESTS AND MEASUREMENTS 165

Test techniques of appraisal
Norms, reliability, validity and standardization
Measurement of Intelligence
Wechsler Intelligence Scales
Measurement of Achievement
Measurement of Aptitudes: SVIB and the Kuder
Measurement of Personality: MMPI
Test Administration and Interpretation
Basic Descriptive Statistics

17. APPRAISAL II: NONTEST TECHNIQUES 186

Observations
Anecdotal records
Rating scales
Pupil data questionnaires
Autobiographies
Diaries
Sociogram
Case study
Cumulative records

18. VOCATIONAL AND CAREER DEVELOPMENT THEORY 194

Factors influencing career development
Types of theories
Eli Ginzberg's general theory
Anne Roe: need theory
Donald Super: self concept theory
John Holland: personality topology
David Tiedeman: teleological model

19. COUNSELING AND GUIDANCE IN THE ELEMENTARY SCHOOL ... 205

Reasons for the development of elementary guidance
Approaches to elementary guidance
Problems of elementary school children
Theoretical approaches with special applicability: play therapy and behavior modification
Differences between elementary and secondary guidance
Areas of controversy

PART IV: SPECIAL TOPICS

20. MENTAL RETARDATION, LEARNING DISABILITIES AND UNDER-ACHIEVEMENT 215

Severe and profound retardation
Mongolism
Cretinism
Microcephaly
Moderate and Mild retardation
Distribution of intelligence
Definition and terminology of learning disabilities
Visual, auditory and motor deficits
Diagnosis and remediation
The role of the counselor

21. THE PROBLEM OF DRUG ABUSE 222

Types of drugs
Contributing and causative factors in drug abuse
Counseling and drug abuse

22. POLITICS, PROTEST AND AUTHORITY 229

The issues
Role of the counselor
Problems for the counselor

23. CONTINUING SOCIAL CRISES 234

The school dropout
Delinquency
Illegitimacy and venereal disease

24. CONTROVERSIES IN COUNSELING AND GUIDANCE 240

Bibliography 245

Index 247

Counseling Psychology
and Guidance

PART **I**

PSYCHOLOGICAL FOUNDATIONS

CHAPTER 1

PSYCHOPATHOLOGY

INTRODUCTION. Psychopathology is the study of abnormal behavior. Clinical psychology and psychiatry have a closer relationship to this field of study than does counseling psychology. In many ways clinical psychology, psychiatry and counseling psychology are differentiated from each other in terms of the *degree* of abnormality or deviancy in the clients or patients treated by each. While there are other important differences between these disciplines, generally psychiatrists and clinical psychologists will treat more severely disturbed patients, and the disorders covered in this chapter will likely be closer to those professions than is the "client" of the counselor. It is important to study psychopathology, however, for at least two reasons: (a) Counselors must know something about the symptomatology of serious psychological disorders to make a tentative diagnosis and an appropriate referral to the professional most competent to treat it. (b) Abnormal behavior is not a black and white affair; some quantitative relationship exists between normal and disturbed. Normal clients often exhibit neurotic and psychotic symptoms at varying times and often show similar kinds of reactions, but their overall integrity is sufficient to continue considering them to be functionally normal. A knowledge of the *abnormal psychology in everyday life*, therefore, is important to the counseling practitioner.

I. DEFINITION OF NORMALCY

There is no magical list and universally accepted group of criteria which spell out the nature and limits of normalcy. Instead, there are a number of definitions. There is overlap and controversy. From the myriad of statements about what is normal, three general approaches may be delineated.

A. Statistical Approach

Certain traits and groups of traits can be quantified and statistically analyzed. Some traits vary significantly from the average or mean of the group. At a certain distance from the average score of performance, one may stipulate that this behavior is "significantly different" from others, that it is atypical. There is a statistical basis, therefore, for claiming that this person, his traits or behavior are abnormal. Classifying a child as mentally defective, for example, is often based upon an IQ score which, in this case, is significantly different from the average IQ in the population. The disadvantage or limitation of the statistical approach, however, is that a genius is also atypical and significantly different from the mean of the population. A statistical criterion alone, therefore, only really separates out differences and typical from atypical traits. Attaching the label of normal or abnormal to these traits is an additional process.

B. Social or Consensual Approach

In the absence of a clear line of direction the best course of action is what the majority of people say it should be. The consensus often determines what is right and within the limits of society, and what is not within those limits. Much behavior is considered normal or abnormal on the basis of whether it conforms to the social system in which it occurs. Killing another human being, for example, is not in itself abnormal in this model; in one society it is murder and the individual is diagnosed as having a character disorder; in another society the individual is a hero and a model for the next generation. Despite its obvious limitations, one cannot ignore the group or society in formulating a definition of normalcy and pathology.

C. Clinical Approach

Research and clinical experience provide a basis for developing a list of criteria, biological, psychological and social, which determine the degree of a person's deviancy or which define whether or not he is normal. This approach depends upon clinical determination and judgment. It obviously suffers from the problems of one expert, with one set of criteria, contradicting another expert with his set of criteria. However, there are some general guidelines which represent this clinical approach and constitute something like a normalcy check list.

1. *Reality Contact.*

The person perceives and reacts appropriately to physical, psychological and social stimuli. He does not, for example, hallucinate.

2. *Competencies and Skills.*

The person has developed certain abilities and coping techniques for dealing with stress and for various problem periods in the chronology of his development.

3. *Self Acceptance.*

The person is able to conceive of himself, is able to picture and reflect upon who he is in the past, present and future, and is able to know of and emotionally accept his positive and negative aspects.

4. *Personality Integration.*

The variety of roles and identities, feelings, and beliefs that an individual experiences during his lifetime are to some degree unified and integrated into his personality. He is relatively free of disabling and mutually contradictory impulses fighting each other in his psyche.

5. *Conformity and Autonomy.*

The individual recognizes and conforms to the requirements of his society, and at the same time he is sufficiently autonomous from these influences not to be their victim.

II. CLASSIFICATION AND INCIDENCE OF PSYCHOPATHOLOGY

The types of abnormal behavior are classified according to a scheme developed by the American Psychiatric Association (1952). Each category will be more thoroughly described later. Figures of incidence are estimates and refer only to the United

States (Coleman, 1964, p. 20). The following is simply an overview of the types of abnormal behavior patterns in broad outline with an approximate estimate of the frequency of each general behavior pattern.

A. Disorders of Psychogenic Origin

1. *Transient Situational Personality Disorders*; 300,000.
2. *Psychoneurotic Disorders*; 10,000,000.
3. *Psychophysiological Disorders*; 20,000,000.
4. *Psychotic Disorders (functional psychosis)*; 700,000.
5. *Personality or Character Disorders*; 3,000,000.

B. Disorders Associated with Organic Brain Disturbance

1. *Acute Brain Disorders*; 100,000.
2. *Chronic Brain Disorders*; 1,000,000.

C. Mental Retardation; 5,500,000

The estimates above do not include problem drinking (5,000,000) nor drug addiction (impossible to estimate at this writing).

III. THE MAJOR FORMS OF PSYCHOPATHOLOGY

Not all forms and subtypes of each category of psychopathology have known or specified causes (etiology). In many cases the psychogenic disorders, those having no apparent physical cause or brain pathology associated with them, are even more ambiguous in terms of understanding their underlying dynamics or causes. Moreover, diagnosing a client and classifying his symptoms into any one of these categories of abnormal behavior is itself often an unreliable and frustrating process and one open to much controversy. Nonetheless, the disorders below are thought to represent relatively homogeneous patterns distinct enough from each other to be considered separately.

A. Disorders of Psychogenic Origin

1. *Transient Situational Personality Disorders.*

Under conditions of acute stress such as war, civilian catastrophes or personal crisis, e.g. the death of a loved one, the resources of the person are depleted, and personality decompensation occurs.

a. *Combat exhaustion.* Soldiers under a continual threat of injury and death, who have maintained a high level of vigilance and physiological mobilization of resources to meet this threat, may gradually deteriorate from such mobilization. They may show signs of dejection, weariness, hypersensitivity, sleep disturbances, tremors and a startle reaction. There is often severe anxiety accompanying the breakdown.

b. *Civilian catastrophes.* While combat exhaustion occurs often under continual and chronic stress, catastrophes which are single, acute traumatic events such as death of a parent or child, explosions, fires, etc., have a different pattern of symptoms associated with them, often called the "disaster syndrome." The individual initially enters a period of *shock* characterized by being stunned, dazed and apathetic, as if in a stupor. As time increases the distance from the trauma, the person moves into a period of *suggestibility*, is passive, follows the directions of others willingly, but still maintains overall inefficient behavior. In neither of these two stages does the person discuss or effectively face what actually happened. Some time later this period of suggestibility is diminished and the person enters a *recovery* phase characterized by retelling the story over and over again, showing much more anxiety and apprehensiveness, having nightmares and difficulty sleeping, etc. This last recovery phase is a cathartic period (Coleman, 1964).

2. *Psychoneuroses.*

Neurotics have a certain general symptomatology and nucleus which is common to most specific neurotic reactions. They tend to have an initial low ability to tolerate external stress, and are characterized by some degree of *anxiety*, tension and irritability. They have a self-centered narcissistic approach to interpersonal relations, tend to lack effective insight and maintain a rigid defensiveness. They are often unhappy and may frequently have somatic complaints. However, they do maintain at least marginal contact with reality and are not victims of any significant delusions or hallucinations.

a. *Anxiety neurosis; anxiety reaction.* Symptoms of this common neurotic disturbance are free floating anxiety, tension, restlessness, difficulty concentrating, insomnia, periodic acute anxiety states and panic accompanied by difficulty breathing. The etiology of the anxiety reaction is thought to rest in some inner conflict perhaps activated by some external threat for which no effective coping techniques have been developed resulting in the panic reaction.

b. *Neurasthenia; asthenic reaction.* The symptoms of this syndrome are chronic mental and physical fatigue, feelings of weakness, lack of vigor, listlessness and often vague somatic complaints. The dynamics of this disorder hypothesize the individual has been under a prolonged frustration or stress leading to discouragement and hopelessness and a feeling that he is too ill to continue the battle, whatever the specific character of that battle may be.

c. *Conversion reaction.* This pattern of symptoms was once called hysteria or conversion hysteria. The person shows signs of neurological impairment, e.g. loss in sensitivity to pain or unusual tingling sensations, paralysis of unusual and often arbitrary portions of the body, choking sensations, etc. What is peculiar is that no organic pathology is associated with any of the symptoms. Moreover, the patient shows a "la belle indifference" or general disinterest in his symptoms. The etiology of the disorder is thought to rest in the repression of certain strong impulses which are not accessible to the awareness of the patient. Hypnosis and certain pharmocological devices have worked successfully in bringing these unconscious conflicts into expression and removing the symptoms.

d. *Obsessive-Compulsive reaction.* These persons are characterized by persistent thoughts, obsessive and irrational sentences, incessant and haunting melodies, etc. Their thinking is ruminative and repetitive. They may have a compulsion to perform some act which appears strange or absurd or to engage in a ritual which is unknown to them. Often, however, they are aware that they are engaging in an activity excessively, e.g. a hand washing compulsion, but are unable to stop it. Obsessive compulsive reactions are interpreted as the individual protecting himself against some internal threat by substitutive action or thought.

e. *Dissociative reaction.* A dissociative reaction is some escape from anxiety arousing internal conflicts by separating or dissociating one aspect of the conflict from the other. There are various types of dissociative reactions which illustrate this dynamic:

(1) Multiple personality. The person assumes two or more identities (Dr. Jekyll and Mr. Hyde).
(2) Amnesia. The person temporarily forgets any details connected with the conflict; severe memory loss.
(3) Fugue. In a fugue state the individual flees from the conflict physically and maintains a state of amnesia during his flight.
(4) Somnambulism. The person carries out some behavior while he is asleep. He acts out some wish while a part of him is unaware of what he is doing.

f. *Phobic reactions.* The individual has fears which he knows are irrational but which cause him much anxiety if he does not obey them. Phobias may be *symbolic*, in that the objects which are feared represent other, more remote, conflicts, or a phobia may be a *conditioned fear response*, originating early in childhood and which is still maintained in adult life. There are many types of phobic reactions: agoraphobia (open places), claustrophobia (closed places), zoophobia (animals), etc.

g. *Neurotic depressive reaction.* This form of psychoneurotic response is quite frequent. The person is characterized by strong feelings of worthlessness, discouragement and fatalism. It is thought that the depressive has had some recent environmental stress or setback which has put into motion an internal self-punitive process resulting in feelings of self-alienation and worthlessness. The depressive often punishes herself instead of directing her aggressive feelings out into the environment or at the source of frustration.

3. *Psychophysiologic Disorders* ("Psychosomatic").

The largest category of abnormal behavioral reactions is found here. The general interpretation for the occurrence of psychophysiological disorders is that we live in an age of stress. As that stress is maintained and the individual unable to adequately cope with it, the biological systems necessary to maintain effective functioning in face of that stress gradually deteriorate. The somatic or organ difficulty is a result of the psychological conflict, thus "psycho-somatic." An amputee who develops a severe depressive reaction, however, would illustrate the reverse causal process, and this would be a "somato-psychic" development. There are countless types of psychosomatic disorders, perhaps limited only to the number of organs which participate in a particular stress reaction. Some of the more common psychophysiological disorders are listed.

a. *Peptic ulcers.* Overly dependent or excessively driving and independent individuals have a higher probability to develop gastrointestinal disturbances such as a peptic ulcer. Sustained hostility or chronic insecurity are thought to be related to the excessive secretion of stomach acid. Under such psychological stress the hyper-acidity ultimately may result in ulceration in the stomach lining, most frequently in the duodenum.

b. *Cardiovascular reactions: Migraine and Hypertension.* Individuals with chronic hostility and feelings of insecurity, who maintain a constant sustained drive or who constantly struggle to obtain some unachievable aim, tend to keep their activity level high and may keep their cardiovascular system in a state of constriction, resulting in hypertension. Individuals who develop migraine, predominantly women, tend to share certain other personality characteristics, e.g. rigidity, obsessiveness, meticulousness, etc. Whatever the content of the emotional tensions, it is thought that the cranial arteries are dilated as a result of these feelings, and that the painful headaches result from these dilations.

c. *Obesity.* Not all obesity is, of course, psychosomatic and this is true of every so-called psychosomatic disorder. However, some people are excessively overweight for psychological reasons; usually overeating may be conceptualized as merely a maladaptive habit, as an activity which serves as a defense against other frustration, or as a protective device which keeps the person from other problems with which he could not cope. For example, a fat person is less likely to be confronted sexually or to have to face the problems of marriage.

d. *Anorexia Nervosa.* Severe loss of appetite typifies this syndrome. It is often related to sexual conflicts or strong dependency needs. The person in many cases ceases taking in enough nutrients for survival, and the disorder may culminate in death if not treated effectively.

e. *Other psychosomatic disorders.* Many other physical difficulties have been related to the psychological stimulus. These include constipation, heartburn, menstrual disturbances, hyperthyroidism, asthma, rheumatism, acne, allergies, muscular cramps, colitis, etc.

4. *Psychotic Disorders: functional psychoses.*

Psychogenic or functional psychosis, i.e. psychosis not apparently related to physical causes but originating from psychological (or social) ones, is distinguished from neurosis in a number of ways. The major difference between the two is given mainly by the degree of contact with reality. Psychotics exhibit *a gross distortion of reality* and are characterized as having *delusions, hallucinations* and *illusions* as well as gross *personality disorganization.* These are not characteristics shared with the psychoneuroses. There are four major types of functional psychosis.

a. *Schizophrenic Reactions.* Schizophrenia is the largest single category of psychotic reaction. While sharing delusions and hallucinations with the other psychoses, it has certain specific symptom patterns: *shallow and blunted emotionality,* unusual and *bizarre gestures* and motor behavior, *disturbances in and interruption of thought processes, preoccupation with inner fantasy life* and a general *withdrawal from reality.* The following basic types of schizophrenia are differentiated.

(1) *Simple Schizophrenia.* Lowered interests, reduced interpersonal relationships, apathy and indifference describe the simple schizophrenic. This reaction is considered a simple form of escape from stress by an overall lowering of emotional functioning.

(2) *Childhood Schizophrenia.* Often disturbed parental relationships accompany childhood schizophrenia. The child shares the general symptom picture of schizophrenia and may have additional autistic or hyperactive components associated with it.

(3) *Hebephrenic Schizophrenia.* This variety of schizophrenia is often quite bizarre with unusual stereotypic behavior, ritualistic mannerisms, nonsensical thought and speech patterns, silliness, inappropriate laughter, and general personality fragmentation and regression. '

(4) *Catatonic Schizophrenia.* Stupor usually characterizes catatonia. The individual may be in a period of hyperactive motor behavior, later to enter a period of generalized motoric inhibition. Here he may not move or alter position for days, but when his position is changed by someone else, he is likely to maintain it, all the time keeping a state of mutism and stupor.

(5) *Paranoid Schizophrenia.* In paranoid schizophrenia, the individual is a victim of hallucinations and strong persecutory delusions or other delusions of reference or omnipotence. He is preoccupied with suspiciousness and hostility and grandiosity. Often his personality disorganization is pronounced.

b. *Paranoid Reactions.* Paranoid reactions are differentiated from schizophrenia and paranoid schizophrenia primarily because they are to some extent specific and discrete elements of the psychotic personality and do not involve the same degree of personality fragmentation and disorganization as in schizophrenia. They are, however, characterized by a significant loss of contact with reality, hallucinations and delusions, and for that reason are treated as psychoses.

(1) *Paranoia.* In this type of paranoid reaction the individual maintains his personality and keeps most of his integrities and competencies relatively high. He is characterized, however, by well systematized delusions, excessive rigidity and suspiciousness, and may maintain a feeling of grandeur or extreme self-importance. It is felt that the

paranoid projects his guilts and feelings of self-punitiveness on to others, imagines that others are tormenting him and feels to some extent stronger and more resolved to continue the fight against such insidious enemies.

(2) *Paranoid State.* A paranoid state, like paranoia itself, is a delusional state with the usual feelings of persecution, grandeur, and suspiciousness with accompanying hallucinations (often auditory). What differentiates it from paranoia, however, is the less systematized structure of the delusions. It does not approach the decompensation and fragmentation of paranoid schizophrenia, but neither does it reach such a high level of detail, systematization, and organization of pure paranoia.

c. *Affective Reactions.* In this category of psychotic disturbance the most distinguishing quality is not the emotional blunting and fragmentation of schizophrenia, nor the suspiciousness and persecutory delusions of paranoid reactions, but the excessive predominance of mood over other factors, whether that be a swing in mood from one pole to the other or a single dominant affective state which proliferates through the mental life of the individual.

(1) *Manic-depressive Reactions.* The person who is manic-depressive swings in mood from exaggerated feeling of optimism, elation, hypomania, hyperactivity, wild flights of ideas, including transient delusions and hallucinations; as well as sometimes extreme delerious mania accompanied by disorientation, violence and destructiveness, to opposite feelings of profound sadness, loneliness and alienation, reduced psychomotor activity, feelings of guilt and regret and often suicidal reactions. Manic-depressive reactions are cyclical, tend to be of short duration, and tend to recur.

(2) *Depressive Reactions.* Depressive reactions show a general retardation of mental and physical activity, loss of appetite, disinterest, pronounced feelings of guilt and unworthiness and suicidal preoccupations. There may be delusions and hallucinations accompanying this reaction.

Feelings of sinfullness, humiliation and worthlessness
are common. Often it is precipitated by outside factors.
Psychotic depressive reactions do not show a cyclical
pattern as in the manic-depressive syndrome.

d. *Involutional Psychotic Reaction*. In this separate depressive
reaction the individual usually does not have a history of
manic-depressive episodes. Involutional psychosis, once
referred to as involutional melancholia, is characterized
by excessive worry, restlessness, insomnia, unprovoked
periods of weeping and hypochondria. There may be
general feelings of hopelessness, self-punishment, guilt
and fatalism, and there may also be other involutional
reactions whose predominant features include paranoid
delusions. These reactions are not as frequently cyclical
as manic depressive reactions and spontaneous recovery
from the illness occurs less often. Onset of involutional
psychosis is usually between the ages of forty and sixty-
five.

5. *Personality or Character Disorders.*

This group of disorders is identified by certain developmental
defects in the personality structure of the individual. These disorders are less often brought about by stress but are more of a
life-long discrete form of pathology. The character disorder is
expressed or acted out in the environment with little or no
anxiety and guilt associated with it. The developmental defects
may be personality traits which have never been cultivated or
manifested in behavior, or may be traits which have undergone
some form of pathological alteration or exaggeration in development. There are four major types of personality disorders.

a. *Special Symptom Reactions*. These reactions are usually discrete behavioral anomalies. Here the specific symptom expresses
the pathology. Some of these disorders are successfully treated
with behavior therapy; others are symptoms which represent
deeper personality conflicts.

(1) *Stuttering*. This disorder varies from mild blocking of
certain speech sounds, e.g. difficulty in pronouncing initial

syllables of words, to more severe contortions where the person is unable to produce initial sounds at all and where head jerks, rapid breathing and facial contortions accompany the blocking. Hereditary, neurological and psychological theories have been forwarded to explain stuttering phenomena.

(2) *Nail-biting.* A great number of individuals bite their finger nails. When this becomes excessive, it enters the area of pathology. Interpretations of nail biting have considered this symptom to be a means of discharging anxiety under stress, an intropunitive form of expressing hostility, or a learned maladaptive habit.

(3) *Tics.* A tic is a persistent muscle spasm. It includes eye blinking, twitching of the mouth, twisting the neck, grimacing, etc. It is usually limited to a distinct muscle group and occurs commonly between six to fourteen years of age, though it is also known to occur among adults. It is alternately interpreted as a means of discharging tension or as some kind of learned maladaptive habit.

(4) *Enuresis.* A child is said to be enuretic if he has an habitual involuntary discharge of urine after the age of three. Enuretic children commonly urinate during deep sleep. This symptom may occur two to fifteen times per week. Enuresis has been interpreted as an indirect expression of hostility or anxiety, a reaction to acute stress, a sign of emotional immaturity, or as a clue to some deeper psychoneurotic disturbance.

(5) *Compulsive Gambling.* The compulsive gambler is distinguished from other individuals who gamble primarily on the basis that it is an irresistable and persistent activity over which the person has little control. Often he places himself and his family in great debt on the belief that soon his luck will change. These individuals tend to share certain personality characteristics, e.g. immaturity, hostility, obsessive and magical cognitive processes, etc.

b. *Personality Pattern Disturbance.* Personality pattern disturbances are basic maladaptive personality types which are rarely altered by traditional psychotherapeutic procedures. Physical abnormalities may be associated with these disturbances. Under acute stress these personalities may decompensate into various forms of psychosis.

(1) *Inadequate Personality.* This individual is characterized by an inadequate response to most demands placed upon him, physical, intellectual and social. He tends to be inept, lack physical and emotional stamina, exercise poor judgment and to be generally incompatible with his peers.

(2) *Schizoid Personality.* The schizoid personality pattern is represented by an inability to express hostility, coldness, avoidance of emotional contact and aloofness. He is often introverted, shy, seclusive and eccentric.

(3) *Cyclothymic Personality.* This personality pattern is a kind of mild manic-depressive pattern, though usually not of psychotic proportions. The person manifests extrovertive tendencies with alternating moods of elation and sadness. These feelings may not be related to any external cues or causes and often occur unpredictably.

c. *Personality Trait Disturbances.* Some individuals have a persistent inability to cope independently with stress. They often lose their emotional balance and tend to be generally immature in terms of personality development. Three types of trait disturbances have been distinguished. Unlike pattern disturbances, trait disorders do not develop into psychosis under acute stress, but rather are characterized by regression and/or exaggeration of these immature characteristics.

(1) *Emotionally Unstable Personality.* This personality trait disturbance is a pattern of emotionality and affectivity which typically results in excessive mood changes, poor judgment, ineffectiveness and often inappropriate expressions of jealousy, envy, hostility, guilt and anxiety, etc.

(2) *Passive-Aggressive Personality.* The passive aggressive personality is typically distinguished as acting out hostile feelings in a passive way, e.g. through stubbornness, ob-

stinacy, pouting, etc. rather than directly or actively. However, it also is meant to include individuals with an extreme need to hold on to others; who are apparently helpless and indecisive. Individuals who are more actively aggressive, but who express their hostility in still-indirect ways, e.g. temper tantrums, irritability, are also included under this rubric.

(3) *Compulsive Personality*. The compulsive personality is rigid, overly conforming, obedient, meticulous and over conscientious.

d. *Sociopathic Personality Disturbance*. This, the largest group of character disorders, includes persons who show an exaggerated lack of conformity to social standards, customs and laws. While there are many forms of deviancy, most fail to develop an adequate sense of social responsibility. Four major groups are distinguished.

(1) *Antisocial Reaction*. The psychopath belongs to this reaction pattern. He is characterized by a lack of ethical development, egocentricity, impulsivity, and a hedonistic attitude toward life. Sometimes he manifests a competent and charming demeanor to others, and this is usually a means of exploiting and manipulating others for personal gain. Most relationships are shallow. Therapy is not particularly successful with the psychopath.

(2) *Dyssocial Reaction*. Dyssocial reaction includes criminals or juvenile delinquents who apparently have intact personality structures and good ego strength but who, at the same time, are the products of environments which themselves are dyssocial. Habitual, aggressive delinquents, for example, who aspire to a criminal career and who receive their social reinforcements through the medium of a juvenile gang would fit this category of character disorder.

(3) *Sexual Deviation*. With changing social standards, it is increasingly difficult to define sexual deviation. However, it is usually a pattern of behavior disapproved by the community and which shows either excessive or retarded

sexual appetite, some abnormality with regard to the sexual "object," or a normal biological sexual pattern occurring, however, under antisocial conditions. Some of the sexual deviations are listed:

- (a) Impotence or frigidity.
- (b) Satyriasis or Nymphomania.
- (c) Promiscuity and prostitution.
- (d) Rape.
- (e) Incest.
- (f) Masturbation.
- (g) Homosexuality.
- (h) Pedophilia.
- (i) Bestiality.
- (j) Exhibitionism.
- (k) Voyeurism.
- (l) Fetishism.
- (m) Pyromania.
- (n) Sadism.
- (o) Masochism.

(4) *Addiction.* Two major forms of addiction are distinguished; addiction to alcohol and to drugs. Forms of alcoholism are many, varying from problem drinking to acute alcoholic hallucinosis. Alcoholism affects some 6% of the adult population in the United States. Chronic alcoholic deterioration shows general personality deterioration, intellectual and moral decline as well as a variety of physical symptoms including tremors, nausea, etc. Alcoholics appear to have a wide ranging variety of personalities, and alcoholism may be accompanied by other forms of psychopathology. Drugs and drug addiction will be treated in subsequent chapters.

B. Disorders Associated with Impairment of Brain Tissue Function

Many diseases or other conditions which affect the central nervous system may give rise to a host of behavioral and emotional disturbances. Often the type, area and extent of neural damage as well as the personality of the patient before the damage occurred is important to understanding the disorder. While these disorders are not psychogenic, there is some indication that a healthy personality can withstand more neural damage than a personality which had "premorbid" signs which may interact with the brain tissue dysfunction to produce the psychopathology.

1. *Acute Brain Disorders.*

An acute brain disorder is one which is transient, temporary and usually reversible. Brain disorders which are the result of high fevers, nutritional deficiencies, intoxication and poisoning, head injuries and tumors are thought to be of this type. Usually there is a diffuse impairment of brain tissue function. Symptoms include delusions and hallucinations, delirium, impaired orientation, memory, judgment, etc.

2. *Chronic Brain Disorders.*

A chronic brain disorder is one in which there is permanent destruction of brain tissue. Some conditions vary from mild disturbance to more severe disturbances. Psychological systems affected are: memory, comprehension, learning, reasoning and emotionality. Some psychological recovery may evidence itself despite the brain dysfunction, depending upon the premorbid personality of the individual and his ability to compensate for the impaired functions brought about by the disorder. Chronic brain disorders arise from a number of causes: birth defects, syphilis, certain types of infection and intoxication, senile brain degeneration, disturbances in circulation, metabolism, growth, etc. Some disorders which have accompanying psychological degeneration are listed below. *These may be either chronic or acute depending upon the specific disorder.* These are just a sampling of some related disorders and do not represent an exhaustive list (Coleman, 1964).

   a. Cerebral syphilis.
   b. Epidemic encephalitis.
   c. Meningitis.

    d. Toxic deliria.

    e. Beri-Beri.

    f. Pellagra.

    g. Hyperthyroidism.

    h. Myxedema.

    i. Addison's disease.

    j. Postpartum psychosis.

    k. Parkinson's disease.

    l. Huntington's chorea.

    m. Alzheimer's disease.

    n. Pick's disease.

    o. Epilepsy.

    p. Senile psychosis.

    q. Arteriosclerotic brain disease.

COMMENTARY: While this chapter roughly followed the American Psychiatric Association classification system, it did so only marginally and does not represent a complete diagnostic classification system by itself. Instead, certain portions of the scheme were selected over others. Chronic undifferentiated schizophrenia, endocrine disorders, musculoskeletal psychophysiologic disorders were just some forms of abnormal behavior patterns which were not treated. Instead, it was the intent of this chapter to provide a broad sketch of psychopathology in sufficient depth without at the same time becoming cumbersome.

The *major* forms of abnormal behavior, however, were treated according to this scheme while their subtypes were at times abbreviated. One other major form of abnormal behavior according to this scheme is Mental Retardation. This has been excluded from this chapter.

Psychopathology is not free of controversy. Whether an obsessive, over conscientious personality is "psychoneurotic, obsessive compulsive reaction" or "personality disorder, personality trait disturbance" is a difficult diagnostic decision which depends upon many other factors and presenting symptoms than described here. Moreover, there are built-in ambiguities in this kind of classification approach, regardless of the diagnostic acuity of the clinician.

While this appears to be the essential core of psychopathology for the school counselor, there are other elements of this discipline which have been neglected. The causes of these disorders (genetic, biological, psychological, social), the types of treatment procedures used for each disorder (chemotherapy, shock therapy, etc.) and the prognosis are just some areas of investigation which ought to be pursued for a more comprehensive look at the study of deviant behavior.

CHAPTER **2**

PERSONALITY THEORY

INTRODUCTION. In psychology personality has come to mean a constellation of personal traits and properties which influence an individual's behavior. It is a dynamic structure which differentiates one man from another. There are indeed many definitions of it and many factors which shape it and determine it. Personality is involved in how well we deal with stress, how we react to anxiety, what cognitive styles we develop to solve problems, what motives push us into activity, how well we maintain control, integration and organization in our lives, as well as how well we express ourselves and live a rich, affective and enjoyable life. In this chapter it is impossible to treat all of the theories of personality, much less to cover those other factors in the study of personality which certainly deserve consideration: e.g. the role of genetic factors, the role of learning, the role of sociocultural factors, etc. Instead, this chapter will present an overview of the important personality theories which shaped counseling theory or which influence it indirectly.

I. SIGMUND FREUD: PSYCHOANALYSIS

Psychoanalysis is both a theory of personality and a technique of therapy. The general theory of psychoanalysis is a highly complex system developed by Freud in the early part of this century. It has influenced clinical thinking with respect to personality and development in countless ways with many of its concepts intact today.

A. Basic Postulates

Psychoanalysis is built upon some fundamental beginning assumptions.

1. *Psychic determinism.*

All mental events are caused. There is no caprice in the mental apparatus, though there is change. All mental activities (thoughts, slips of the tongue, nonsensical speech) are related to other factors in causal and regular ways.

2. *Empiricism.*

Psychoanalysis is rooted in observation and experience. Its theories are based upon observations and subject to change on the basis of contradictory observations. It is not metaphysical or philosophical but fundamentally a scientific discipline.

3. *Reductionism.*

The organism develops in a hierarchical way. Early experience is more significant than later experience. As such, most mental events in the life of an adult may be traced back, reduced or analyzed into simpler, more basic psychological elements and conflicts.

4. *Equilibrium and Homeostasis.*

The organism seeks to restore a state of equilibrium and balance. It strives to reduce tensions and in this process experiences pleasure.

B. Instincts

All behavior is motivated, and it is motivated by what Freud described as "drive" or instincts. Instincts are biological in origin but release mental energy; as such they are a link between mental and physical worlds. Some of the major elements of the theory of instincts are given.

1. *Eros.*

The general name given to the life instincts, Eros, includes those drives which govern the lives of all organisms.

a. *Self Preservative instincts.* Life instincts whose major function is to preserve the life of the individual are referred to as self-preservative or ego instincts. Examples are hunger, thirst, needs for air, etc.

b. *Sexual instincts.* Sexual instincts are ultimately concerned with the propogation and *preservation of the species* and not necessarily the preservation of the individual. These forces are more flexible than self preservative instincts in that they may be delayed or suspended from their object of gratification for indefinite periods while self-preservative instincts are more pressing drive states seeking immediate gratification.

2. *Thanatos.*

The life instincts, Eros, bind elements and unite them. Freud postulated another major instinct, one which aims at unbinding and destruction. All living things are reduced to an inorganic state and the purpose of all life is to return to such a state. Thanatos, the death wish or death instinct, is the name given to this drive and to man's tendency toward self-destruction.

C. Psychosexual Development

Life instincts provide the source of energy for the entire mental apparatus, the *libido.* Personality develops parallel to the organization of the libido. Libidinal organization follows certain stages and tends to fixate in various erogenous zones as the child progresses to adulthood.

1. *Oral phase.*

The infant relates to the external world through his mouth. Is is through this erogenous zone that survival and gratification are found. The mother's breast is the first object of reality which the infant experiences and it is, thus, the first object of sexual or libidinal desire.

2. *Anal phase.*

From ages 2 to 3 the child develops increasing muscular control. It is at this period that he learns to retain and expel waste materials. Libidinal gratification in both retentive and expulsive functions characterizes the anal phase of development.

3. *Phallic phase.*

From 3 to 5 years of age for boys (somewhat later for girls) the child finds pleasure in the manipulation of the genitals. The major locus of the libido has passed from oral and anal erogenous zones to the genitals. Masturbation is common.

4. *Latency period.*

From ages 6 to 12 it is said that sexual interests decline as the child concentrates or sublimates his libido to the acquisition of appropriate skills, competencies, and a preliminary sexual identity (masculine or feminine). This waning of sexuality is termed the latency period and is thought to be precipitated by the resolution of the Oedipus complex (see D).

5. *Genital period.*

After puberty, the genitals become the full focus of sexuality, providing that development has not been retarded or fixated at earlier stages. Appropriate patterning of heterosexual relations and adult sexuality is achieved gradually through adolescence into adulthood.

D. The Oedipus Complex

During the phallic period of psychosexual development the young boy is said to direct his sexual strivings towards his mother in the form of an incestuous wish. Cultural and familial forces are exerted to discourage these impulses. The boy is said to see his father as a competitor and a rival for his mother's love. He fears his father and develops a specific fear called *castration anxiety*. The male Oedipus complex is resolved by the boy's *repression* of his incestuous strivings for his mother and his forming an alliance with his father, a kind of apprentice relationship, where he wishes to become like his father and to identify with him. He enters the period of *latency,* therefore, renouncing his sexual feelings for his mother, and learning progressively how to become a man like his father.

The female Oedipus complex is more complex. The young girl must replace her libidinal attachments for her mother with sexual strivings for the male. The girl does this by developing a desire to have or possess a penis (the female analogue to the clitoris or female phallic erogenous zone). She develops *penis envy* which is a feeling directed toward her father and is competitive and jealous of her mother. The girl resolves her Oedipus complex (sometimes referred to as the *Electra Complex*) by replacing the wish for a penis by a wish for a child (the achievement of genital sexuality).

E: Topographic Position

The psychosexual theory or libido theory is often termed the *economic* position in psychoanalytic theory in that it refers to economy of mental energy available in the mental apparatus. The topographic position of psychoanalytic theory refers to its trichotomy of levels of awareness.

1. *The Unconscious.*

Through his observations of hypnotic phenomena and hysteria, Freud felt a need to develop a system which included memories and experiences which were not accessible to the individual. These unconscious layers of mental life, particularly the preverbal experiences of childhood, remain in the mental apparatus and condition our conscious lives and perceptions, but are fundamentally inaccessible to our awareness. The unconscious is a very large portion of our mental lives, and its contents are noticeable to some degree in dreams.

2. *The Preconscious.*

One of the surface layers of the unconscious is the preconscious; this layer of awareness includes those experiences and memories which are not immediately accessible to awareness but with some minimal effort will come into consciousness. Preconscious experiences can be recalled.

3. *Consciousness.*

The smallest province of mental life is conscious. Consciousness is what the individual is aware of at a given moment.

F. Structural Position

Freud attempted to describe the structure of personality in terms of three basic mental agencies with different functional properties.

1. *Id.*

The id is a subsystem of personality which is all that is present at birth. The id contains all of the instincts which are inherited, and it operates purely hedonistically seeking to reduce tensions and gratify them immediately (the pleasure principle). Man's primitive and forbidden impulses are contained in the id. The id is entirely unconscious.

2. *The Ego and its defenses.*

The ego develops gradually and is concerned with self-preservation. It attempts to mediate between the demands of the id and the external world which might satisfy those needs. The ego operates according to the *reality principle;* it is rational. It *perceives* the external world, stores up *memories* about it, attempts to master it and to develop appropriate problem-solving competencies to function effectively in it. The ego controls motility and, as such, it controls the access the id has to gratification of impulses. The character of the ego defines to what degree the individual has "reality contact." In neurotic and psychotic disorders the ego has lost such reality contact and is fragmented to a considerable degree.

To some degree the ego is unconscious. It often defends itself from impulses originating in the id. It does this by utilizing a *signal of anxiety* which warns it of impending danger. In order to address and reduce anxiety, the ego employs a number of defense mechanisms which protect it from access into consciousness of certain undesirable feelings and impulses. The character of the ego is often described in terms of the predominant types of defenses the individual employs. Some of these defensive patterns are listed.

a. *Repression.* The basic mechanism of defense the ego employs against impulses which cause anxiety is to exclude them entirely from consciousness. The individual refuses to see or recognize various motives he may have which elicit anxiety. This process of exclusion from consciousness is called repression.

b. *Regression.* Another defense an individual may use to protect himself is to return to earlier tried and safe behavior patterns which may be characteristic of a less mature developmental period. Thumb sucking in elementary school children who have difficulty adjusting to school may be an example of this regressive behavior.

c. *Denial.* A primitive defense mechanism, denial is a simple refusal to admit an aspect of reality. It is a kind of head-in-the-sand escapism from externally threatening stimuli.

d. *Reaction-formation.* The protective reaction involves turning the threatening impulse into its opposite. A militant crusader against pornography may have strong sexual needs of a voyeuristic nature. This kind of reversal of the impulse into its opposite is the means by which the true nature of the impulse is disguised.

e. *Projection.* Threatening impulses are directed outward, in projection, and attributed to someone else rather than the individual himself. A person with strong unresolved homosexual inclinations may see others attempting to make homosexual advances toward him. Here his homosexual impulse is said to be *projected* onto the other person.

f. *Undoing.* Undoing is a form of atonement which is designed to reverse or wipe away some forbidden act or impulse. Apologizing, doing penance, confessing or repenting are forms of undoing. Undoing provides the individual with an outlet for otherwise severe guilt feelings and lowered self-esteem.

g. *Rationalization.* A mild form of protective maneuver is to attribute the cause of some act as different from the true motives that lead up to it. Other reasons, sometimes quite plausible, are given rather than the true reasons and motives behind the act.

h. *Other mechanisms.* Much has been devoted to so-called "ego psychology" in terms of the elaboration and identification of various defense mechanisms. Such mechanisms as *identification, introjection, displacement, sublimation, isolation,* are additional means of dealing with threatening impulses and are worthy of more detailed study.

3. *The Superego.*

The third major personality structure is the superego. This agency of mental functioning is the precipitate of the values of the culture and effectively represents the individual's conscience.

Conscience is developed through interaction within the family primarily by way of identification with the child's parents. Man's social feelings are represented by the superego. The source of his guilts are found here also. The superego exerts pressure on the ego to restrain and inhibit impulses arising from the id. In the asocial personality, the individual may be impulsive and criminal; here the superego may be inadequately developed. On the other hand, an inhibited fearful neurotic may be plagued with anxiety as a result of an excessively strong superego which forbids any release of instinctual energy and forces the ego to become rigid, inflexible and overcontrolled (Brenner, 1955).

II. CARL JUNG: ANALYTIC PSYCHOLOGY

Jung was originally a student of Freud's who later broke with traditional or orthodox psychoanalysis to formulate his own analytic psychology. The basic elements of his system are presented below.

A. Purposivism and Determinism

Jung takes a dualistic position on the causes of human behavior. The psyche is a result of the past, on the one hand, and it shapes its own future and destiny on the other. Jung, therefore, accepts both a teleological (purposive) and deterministic position on the nature of human behavior.

B. The Libido

Freud confined the definition of the libido to be a sexual energy which governed the mental apparatus. Jung used libido as a general energy concept, a life energy. Libido may be used for sexual pursuits or it may energize cultural or creative activities.

C. The Unconscious

Jung enlarged Freud's concept of the unconscious. The unconscious shapes and conditions behavior. It is divided into two agencies or provinces.

1. *Personal unconscious.*

The personal unconscious contains forgotten and repressed experiences, fantasies and dreams, and "complexes" in the life of the individual e.g. the drive for power, the Oedipus conflict, etc. These complexes are strong constellations of psychic energy.

2. *Collective unconscious.*

Man holds the memories not only of his own experiences but of those of the race. Ancestral experiences belong to the individual through the collective unconscious. Similarities in mythology and folklore between disparate cultures are explained by the collective psyche. Inside the collective unconscious are *archetypes*, universal images which correspond to significant emotional elements in the life of man. One's image and conception of his mother is conditioned by his experience with his own mother (personal unconscious) as well as one's remembrance of the primeval image of a universal or eternal mother (the archetype).

D. Consciousness

The third part of the psyche is the conscious mind. Consciousness is concerned with adaptation in fine detail. It is made up of the ego, and the individual sees it as the center of his world and being. It provides the individual with a sense of continuity and identity, but it is miniscule in comparison with the unconscious and it derives its integrity and power only as it relates to the unconscious. The individual can only attain integration and unity in his life as he tries to integrate forces in the unconscious with the adaptive characteristics of the conscious ego. Disturbances arise when one is cut off from the other.

E. Complexes

A complex is a bundle of psychic energy which acts in a somewhat autonomous way within the personality. It is not within the control of the conscious ego. There are various forms of complexes.

1. *Persona.*

The persona is the mask each individual wears to play the roles required of him by society. A man is a father, a husband and an employee, and each of these roles requires him to adopt a particular style of feeling and behavior. When the ego identifies too strongly with the persona, the individual loses contact with his own identity, in favor of the roles ascribed to him. This loss of contact cuts him off from his unconscious influences and he becomes less of an individual and a human being in so doing.

2. *Shadow.*

Primitive animal instincts and forbidden impulses gather together in the unconscious to form the shadow. The shadow is the opposite of the ego and represents all of the opposites the ego identifies with and incorporates as itself. The over assertive man for example would have submerged submissive and receptive impulses as his shadow.

3. *Anima/Animus.*

Another unconscious complex is the anima or animus. Each individual is bi-sexual, secreting both sex hormones. Masculinity emerges in the male through learning and maturation, but the feminine influences in his sexual identity are also present. The feminine quality in the male is called the *anima.* The masculine quality of the female is called the *animus.* The anima and animus are archetypes and represent racial conceptions of masculinity and femininity. When a man does not remain in contact with his opposite-sexed counterpart, the anima, this complex will have disturbing consequences in marital life. They will become contents of the shadow and plague him by threatening to break through into his conscious life or by causing him to distort others by seeing his forbidden impulses in them.

4. *The Self.*

The self may or may not emerge in the person's life. It represents a new center of personality, somewhere between the conscious and unconscious psyche. It is the goal of life and represents an integrating force between the conscious and unconscious elements of personality. It is a larger concept than ego, and it is not synonymous with it. The self, through the process of individuation, strives to free itself from the influences of the *persona* on the one hand, and from unconscious images on the other. Personality integration is achieved through the development of the self which attempts to *transcend* the different systems and unite them into a whole unit. It is usually achieved later in one's life.

5. *Personality types.*

Libido may be directed inwardly (introversion) or outwardly (extroversion). Life energy, moreover, may be considered in terms of two processes, rational and irrational. Jung identified two rational processes (thinking and feeling) and two irrational processes (sensation and intuition). A combination of all of these elements and a dominance of one trait over another defines and generates the various personality types (Wolman, 1960).

a. *Extroverted Thinking Type.* This person utilizes logical analysis in order to construct his reality. He is concerned with facts and their organization.

b. *Extroverted Feeling Type.* This person feels in response to some external circumstance; he is able to establish meaningful social relationships and friendships with others; he feels and acts according to the demands placed upon him.

c. *Extroverted Sensation Type.* This individual is oriented to sensory impressions of a concrete nature; he is specific, a realist and a materialist.

d. *Extroverted Intuition Type.* Here external stimulation only offers the individual appropriate inuendo for understanding what is occurring outside. The individual intuits what ought to be done or understood in the external context.

e. *Introverted Thinking Type.* The individual is cognitive and insular; his thinking is highly subjective.

f. *Introverted Feeling Type.* The person lives in his own world of fantasies and day dreams; he has his own internal web of emotions.

g. *Introverted Sensation Type.* The "impressionist" character who is aware of the external world but whose sensations are colored by his subjective state would fit this personality category.

h. *Introverted Intuition Type.* This person gives his attention to imagery and lives within his own world of understandings. He may be a religious personality.

III. ALFRED ADLER: INDIVIDUAL PSYCHOLOGY

Adler was once associated with Freud but broke with his ideas early in the development of psychoanalysis. His disagreement was somewhat more drastic than Jung's, and his system developed in more unorthodox ways. Some basic principles are worth noting.

A. Teleology

Man is not a product of a cause and effect sequence. Personality theory is not mechanistic. Instead, every psychic phenonema of man is goal-directed and purposeful. What makes it understandable is not what caused it, but where it is leading. Teleology is the first principle of individual psychology.

B. Uniqueness of the Individual

Each man is unique and must be understood in his own experience. No individuals are the same. Each individual is shaped by heredity and environment, but there is a third force, the *creative power* which influences one's movement toward overcoming obstacles in his life's path. The manner in which the individual moves through his life in his uniqueness; his utilization of his free, creative power to carve out his own style of life. This power is not reducible to biological force as is the libido of psychoanalysis.

C. Aggressive Drive

Originally Adler considered the basic driving force in man to be an aggressive drive, a 'will to power.' Later he changed his system and instead postulated that the basic energizing force was a drive for *perfection* or *completion*; in this sense a drive which *strives towards becoming.* Neurotic derivatives of this basic drive are the drive for power or personal superiority, aggressive or anti-social drives, etc. Pleasure or displeasure are secondary rewards to this drive for completion.

D. Inferiority Complex

Man comes into the world in a state of helplessness and inferiority. The goal of life is to overcome inferiorities, to compensate for them and to strive for security, power and perfection. The major force governing man's life is to overcome his inferiority through a continuous striving for superiority.

E. Fictional Finalism

People develop certain thoughts about consequences or goals to be sought. They orient themselves, their feelings and their behavior toward reaching these goals. The goals themselves are subjective states (fictional) which teleologically motivate behavior. So many habits and behaviors are interwoven in this striving or goal-directed process that the individual himself may not be fully aware of the final goal for which he strives. The fictional goal is, in one sense, determined by his specific inferiorities and, on the other, it is a principle of unity and integrity in his behavior which defines his individuality. The fictional goals may be in part unconscious.

F. Life Style

The life style of an individual is his basic "inner core" exemplified in his constant movement toward the fictional final goal. The style of life influences all vital manifestations; it is the central indivisible motif of personality. A person's life style is uniquely his own and never duplicated by another person.

G. Social Interest and Social Embeddedness

The development of appropriate social interest determines largely the degree to which an individual is neurotic. Social interest implies a concern with other persons. The child first directs social interest towards its mother; gradually it spreads out to father, siblings, relatives and ultimately mankind. If one's social embeddedness becomes retarded or interrupted, disordered, anti-social or narcissistic behavior is an ultimate result. Social interest tempers the drive for superiority and makes it a productive, creative and useful drive rather than a selfish, acquisitive drive for power (Ansbacher & Ansbacher, 1956).

IV. ERIK ERIKSON: IDENTITY AND THE EIGHT AGES OF MAN

Erikson's work is not usually considered personality theory per se in the literature. However, it is cited to such an extent as it relates to developmental and ego psychology that its inclusion here is necessary. Erikson sees personality development as a process of achieving a meaningful ego-identity, a kind of "self-sameness." The individual interacts with his environment and reaches eight crisis points in which important psychological issues and instinctual energies are resolved. The way each of these crisis points is interfaced determines the kind of identity the individual will achieve and determines how he will interact with subsequent crises. The eight ages of man are abstracted below (Erikson, 1950).

A. Basic Trust Vs. Basic Mistrust

The infant learns to sense that there will be continuity and predictability in his environment. This sense of trust is communicated by his mother. It results in a feeling of being good-in-the-world. Irregular and discontinuous maternal relations in the first year of life may result in a sense of suspicion or unpleasantness in the world.

B. Autonomy Vs. Shame and Doubt

During toilet training years, the child develops increasing muscular control in bowel and bladder elimination. Parental pressures for the child to develop this control and become autonomous and self-sufficient in performing these functions brings the child to his second crisis stage. Appropriate and flexible training can provide the child with a sense of competence, independence and self-esteem. Excessive disparagement or shaming may lead to lack of self-confidence, obstinacy and self-doubt.

C. Initiative Vs. Guilt

The child developing motoric and language skills may approach a wider choice of activities. As he expands outward with his curiosities, he may confront situations which he is frightened by, which are unexplainable or which cause a sense of guilt. The child leaves this period able to deal with his fears, jealousies and hatreds somewhat openly so that he can actively approach and interact with his environment. Where these fears and hatreds overwhelm him and are reinforced by parental disapproval, the child may develop a debilitating sense of guilt.

D. Industry Vs. Inferiority

The child develops skills and competencies which are basic to his relationship to the world. In this intense immersion into the world of things and tools, the child develops a sense of mastery and industry through effective parental reinforcement, or he experiences frustration and failure resulting in a more generalized feeling of inferiority and incompetence.

E. Identity Vs. Role Diffusion

The onset of puberty upsets previous psychological gains in terms of who one is, what one will be, the difference between "man" and "boy" etc. Doubts about sexual identity must be resolved and heterosexual interests clarified. The danger of this period is the failure to develop an image of self and what one wishes to become, i.e. role diffusion.

F. Intimacy Vs. Isolation

Developing a sense of self leads to confidence in approaching social relationships and developing close and intimate contacts with others. Where roles and self-concepts are weakly developed, the individual may fear involvement since it threatens ego boundaries and withdraw into isolation and insularity.

G. Generativity Vs. Stagnation

Entering this middle period of life the individual is concerned with creative productivity and spreading altruistic social interests and concern for mankind. Failure to develop a healthy sense of contribution and self-value may result in meandering stagnation and lack of fulfilment.

H. Ego Integrity Vs. Despair

This closing period of maturity is characterized by the individual's belief in himself and in his contributions, a self satisfaction and reward. Loss of this feeling results in depression, despair, hostility, contempt and regret.

V. CARL ROGERS: PERCEPTUAL-PHENOMENOLOGICAL THEORY OF PERSONALITY

Roger's systematic development of the client-centered viewpoint in counseling has resulted in a unique approach to the discussion of personality and personality development. Some critical concepts of his theory of personality are given here (Patterson, 1966). Major concepts are underlined. More systematic development of his therapeutic model is discussed in the chapter on counseling systems and theories.

A. Infancy

The individual exists in a field of experience of which he is the center. The *phenomenal field* is entirely subjective and unique to the individual. It is a private world of experience; no individual's experience corresponds exactly to any other's. When the infant enters the world, his experience is reality; he reacts to it wholistically. The infant seeks to *actualize* itself, i.e. to develop all of its capacities in order to maintain and enhance itself.

B. Development of Self

Through experience and interaction with others, the infant gradually begins to define his own boundaries and recognize the difference between "me" and "it." Part of his experience becomes symbolized as self-experience; he becomes an object in his own experiential field. Self emerges.

C. Need for Positive Regard

The child's awareness of Self is, in part, determined by his experiences with others who perceive him. In this interaction

with his parents and significant "others" he develops a need for
their valuing of him, i.e. a need for their positive regard, since,
to some degree, his Self is contingent upon their positive perception of him.

D. The Need for Self Regard

The child's need for positive regard results in either a satisfaction or a frustration of this need. The precipitate of this
satisfaction or frustration is the Self. The Self, as such, begins
to value itself or not to value itself as a result of this experience.
The child begins to like himself as he experiences others liking
him; further he begins to need his own self-valuing as he develops.

E. Developing Conditions of Worth

Certain experiences of the child are valued by "significant
others" while others are not. The child's valuing of himself,
therefore, tends to become contingent. In essence, conditions
are established in which the child recognizes that he is more
or less worthy of positive regard.

F. Developing Incongruence between Self and Experience

Inasmuch as some experience is contingent, it is more or less
compatible with the Self. Positive experiences tend to be incorporated in Self-experience, whereas negative experiences tend
to be denied symbolization in awareness or distorted. The Self
is no longer *congruent* with its experience. When there is incongruence between self and experience as a result of these conditions of worth, the individual becomes vulnerable and experiences threat.

G. Developing Discrepancies in Behavior

Incongruence between Self and experience ultimately culminate in discrepancies in behavior; some behaviors belong to the
individual, and others are so sufficiently distorted or denied that
they are not incorporated into the self concept.

H. Experience of Threat and the Process of Defense

As incongruence develops and behavioral discrepancies result, the individual becomes vulnerable to threat. In order to prevent anxiety, a defensive process is set in motion. Perception is reduced and made more rigid and inflexible. A narrowing of the experiential field occurs.

I. Breakdown and Disorganization

The individual experiences considerable anxiety as his incongruence is heightened. When a significant experience occurs which cannot be satisfactorily defended, the individual behaves inconsistently. The self-structure becomes disorganized.

J. Reintegration

In order for a reintegration of self with experience to occur, the fundamental incongruence must be decreased. Since incongruence developed as a result of the individual experiencing *conditions of worth,* it is thought if the individual experiences unconditional positive regard from a significant other (e.g. a therapist) that he will experience unconditional self-regard, and as a result, he will become congruent with his experience. The individual has a natural synthetic tendency to reintegrate and to become whole. In a permissive and accepting atmosphere where conditions are not attached to the individual's own valuing process, the individual will naturally reintegrate self and experience as part of the self-actualizing tendency.

COMMENTARY. There are trait-factor, constitutional and sociological approaches to personality theory which have relevance to counseling but, for reasons of brevity, have not been treated. Furthermore, research on personality and its effects on behavior is exhaustive. Personality deserves more in depth study by students who are developing and clarifying their own counseling approaches. The theories of Freud, Jung, Adler, Erikson and Rogers, however, tend to be most often cited in the literature and should provide the student with at least a sketch of the important concepts which need to be addressed in conceptualizing a meaningful personal counseling model.

CHAPTER **3**

THE PSYCHOLOGY OF LEARNING

INTRODUCTION. If psychology itself can claim to be a science, it is the psychology of learning which has given it this right. Research in learning has evolved in this century to a high degree of technological and methodological sophistication. Many of the experimental techniques found in personality and social research are directly taken from designs and procedures worked out in learning laboratories. The purpose of this chapter is to give a short introduction to some of the more basic concepts, terms and theories of learning.

I. DEFINITION OF LEARNING

In general, learning is considered a change from some past behavior to some new behavior that is not due to some other factors like growth, maturation, injury, etc. Much controversy is involved around exactly what to call learning. Some more representative definitions are given.

A. **Learning is a change in performance occurring under conditions of practice**

B. **Learning is a change in behavior not attributable to maturation, injury or disease**

C. **Learning is a strengthening in the bond between a stimulus and a response**

D. **Learning is an internal process which is inferred from changes in behavior**

II. BASIC CONCEPTS IN LEARNING

There are various types of learning situations each carrying

42

with it its own peculiar terminology. There are, however, some basic concepts which have a wide generality across these various types of learning paradigms. Many of the "basic laws of learning" depend upon the type of learning situation which is used. Most basic concepts in learning are found within these distinct learning paradigms (Hall, 1966).

A. Conditioned-Response Learning (Classical Conditioning)

Ivan Pavlov is most responsible for bringing classical conditioning phenomena to the attention of psychologists. If food is placed on a dog's tongue it salivates. This is an unlearned reflex. If, at the time the food is presented, a bell rings, it is possible, subsequently, to cause the dog to salivate purely by ringing the bell in the absence of any food. When this new, arbitrary stimulus elicits salivation, classical conditioning is said to have been demonstrated. The reflex of salivation has been conditioned to a neutral stimulus and is elicited by it; it is then a conditioned reflex, a learned one. Some terminology of classical conditioning is given.

1. *Unconditioned Stimulus* (UCS).

Any stimulating situation which evokes an unconditioned response is called an unconditioned stimulus. In the example above, the food placed in the dog's mouth is the unconditioned stimulus.

2. *Unconditioned Response* (UCR).

The response which is elicited by the USC is called the unconditioned response. The salivation of the dog after presentation of the food would be an example.

3. *Conditioned Stimulus* (CS).

Any stimulating state of affairs which the organism discriminates and which is presented with the unconditioned stimulus is called the conditioned stimulus. The stimulus may be arbitrary or neutral to the organism originally. It is, however, presented or paired in some way with the UCS. For example, when the food (UCS) is placed in the dog's mouth, a bell rings (CS).

4. *Conditioned Response* (CR).

The response elicited by a conditioned stimulus is called a conditioned response. When the unconditioned response (salivation) is now elicited solely by the conditioned stimulus (the bell ringing) in the absence of the unconditioned stimulus (food), this response is now called a conditioned response.

5. *Other Terminology.*

Conditioned response learning occurs when the new stimulus (CS) evokes the previously reflexive response. There are many types of conditioning, some more effective in producing conditioned response learning than others.

a. *Delayed conditioning.* The CS appears prior to the UCS and terminates with the onset of the UCS.

b. *Simultaneous conditioning.* The CS appears and terminates with the UCS.

c. *Trace conditioning.* The CS is presented and terminated prior to the onset of the UCS.

d. *Temporal conditioning.* The UCS is presented at regular intervals.

e. *Backward conditioning.* The CS occurs after the USC terminates.

A.   Instrumental Conditioning

Another form of conditioning or learning is the instrumental situation. Here it is necessary for the organism to perform some act or response in order to receive a reward. The reinforcing state of affairs is contingent upon the organism's behavior. A child, for example, who is fed (rewarded) each time that he cries (response), is likely in the future to cry in order to obtain that reward. Here crying is the instrumental response. There are many types of instrumental learning situations. Two varieties are of particular interest.

1. *Avoidance Conditioning.*

Some instrumental conditioning involves the use of negative stimulus situations where noxious reinforcements are given. The organism must avoid the negative state of affairs and may do so either actively or passively. The study of the effects of punishment and negative reinforcement often use this conditioning model.

a. *Active avoidance conditioning.* Also called escape conditioning, the organism is presented with a conditioned stimulus, e.g. a buzzer rings, followed by an unconditioned stimulus (an electric shock). Some interval of time intervenes between the CS and UCS. In order to avoid the UCS, or the negative reinforcement, the organism performs some instrumental response to escape the situation (e.g. presses a bar to terminate the shock or jumps out of the shock area entirely).

b. *Passive avoidance conditioning.* In this situation the organism must avoid performing a previously learned response in order to escape the noxious stimulus. Its failure to respond (passive) is instrumental in avoiding punishment.

2. *Operant Conditioning.*

This learning situation has been most extensively developed by *B. F. Skinner.* Operant conditioning is a form of learning in which responses are emitted by the organism for certain stimulus consequences (reinforcements), not in response to any known previous stimulation. An operant response is one which is already in the behavioral repertoire of the organism. It occurs at a certain frequency. Learning may be said to be a change in the frequency of operant responding. What controls the frequency of response emission is a certain pattern of reinforcement, or reinforcement schedule. Further elaboration of operant conditioning is found in some of the more basic concepts listed below.

a. *Reinforcement.* A reinforcement is anything which affects the frequency or rate of emission of an operant. If, for example, an animal presses a bar to receive a food pellet, the food operates as a reinforcer in that it affects the frequency of bar pressing (operant). Reinforcements are specific to the organism. Praise and blame may operate as reinforcements for humans, but would not be effective reinforcers for infrahuman organisms.

b. *Shaping.* Sometimes new responses are created out of old ones, or certain responses achieve a higher degree of elaboration and specification than others, e.g. aiming a gun. As a response is repeated, it may be reinforced successively as it gradually approximates this ideal or goal. The process of reinforcing a response as it gradually approximates the ideal response pattern is called shaping.

c. *Reinforcement schedules.* The way an organism responds and the rate at which it responds is controlled by the schedule of reinforcement that it is operating under. Four major types of reinforcement schedules have been differentiated.

(1) *Fixed Interval* (FI). The first response which is made after some fixed period of time, is reinforced. For example, the animal is given a food pellet as soon as it presses a bar, after a period of two minutes has elapsed from its last rewarded bar press.

(2) *Variable Interval* (VI). The first response made after some variable period of time, is reinforced. The animal is rewarded on its first response after a two minute, then a four minute interval, then a two minute interval, etc.

(3) *Fixed Ratio* (FR). The first response made after some fixed number of responses is reinforced, e.g. the animal is reinforced with a food pellet after each tenth bar press.

(4) *Variable Ratio* (VR). The first response made after some variable number of responses is reinforced. The animal is reinforced after each tenth press, then after each thirteenth bar press, etc.

C. Other General Learning Concepts

There are some concepts in learning which are widely used in varying types of learning situations. Some familiarity with their meaning is essential.

1. *Primary Reinforcement.*

Usually primary reinforcement is defined as something which reduces a primary need, e.g. food, water, etc.

2. *Secondary Reinforcement.*

A stimulus that is somehow associated with a primary reinforcement becomes a secondary reinforcer. For example, a hungry child is fed and food serves as the primary reinforcer. However, he is fed in the presence of another stimulus, his mother, and his mother becomes reinforcing herself, i.e. she takes on secondary reinforcing properties.

3. *Extinction.*

When reinforcement is stopped, the learned response declines in frequency or ceases to occur. This process is called experimental extinction. In classical conditioning, when the conditioned stimulus loses its properties of evoking the conditioned response, the CR is said to have been extinguished.

4. *Spontaneous Recovery.*

After extinction has occurred, a sufficient lapse of time will occur after which the organism will spontaneously recover from extinction and perform the response previously extinguished. In classical conditioning terms, this means that the CS which no longer elicited the CR will again elicit the CR after a certain passage of time even though the UCS is never presented again.

5. *Stimulus Generalization.*

A response which was elicited by a certain stimulus can also be elicited by a similar but different stimulus. A child who is bitten by a dog may subsequently fear not only dogs, but all animals. Here the fear-eliciting stimulus has been generalized.

6. *Discrimination.*

Sometimes considered antithetical to stimulus generalization, discrimination refers to the ability of the organism to respond to one stimulus and not respond to another, perhaps highly similar stimulus. Discrimination-training is often used in psychotherapeutic practice. As in the previous example, a widely generalized fear reaction can be reduced as other similar stimuli are introduced which do not elicit that response. The child is taught to discriminate birds from dogs, then cats from dogs, etc., until his fear is only elicited by dogs. He discriminates between dogs and other animals and his phobia is less pronounced as a result.

7. *Social Learning.*

Humans may parallel animals only to some extent. Generalizations from infrahuman organisms' learning patterns are valid only to that extent. Reinforcement patterns tend to be different at a social level. Attention, love, respect, praise or money may operate as positive social reinforcers which may not be effective with other organisms. Much research in this kind of human social learning has developed. Recently it has centered upon *imitative* or *vicarious learning,* where a child *models* behavior which he has seen performed and reinforced, but has not performed the behavior and been reinforced himself. Imitative learning may be a way of acquiring new response patterns which are not comprehensively explained purely by classical conditioning or operant conditioning approaches. Aggressive behavior, for example, may occur less because it is gradually "shaped" through various reinforcement schedules, but because the child is imitating or modeling an adult who has performed those responses and has been reinforced for doing so.

III. THEORIES OF LEARNING

A number of efforts have been forwarded to explain the phenomena of learning and to postulate what the basic and elemental factors are which produce it. The role of drive and motivation; the role of practice, the role of association, the role of cognition, insight and expectancies have all participated in these theoretical controversies. It is considered beyond the scope of this outline to treat exhaustively all of the learning theories in the depth they deserve. Rather, a general summary is provided for each so that the student can at least pick up the flavor of the theoretical point of view (Wolman, 1960).

A. Contiguity Theory (Edwin Guthrie)

Guthrie's position tends to place practice or frequency in learning in a secondary role. Instead, he feels learning is a one-trial affair, a form of *simultaneous conditioning.* A stimulus which acts at the *time* of response in the organism, or which is *con-*

tiguous with the response, has a higher probability of evoking that response the next time it occurs. The basic law of learning, then, is the contiguity between stimulus and response. A response is improved with practice, not because it is continually strengthened, as some frequency theorists explain, but, because increasing numbers of stimuli are used as conditioners, each attaching themselves to the response complex on a one-trial basis. Improved performance which "appears" to be due to practice, therefore, is explained rather as a series of discrete discontinuous S-R associations which appear to pile up upon each other. Extinction is explained similarly. In contiguity theory, learning is a single event, and it is not a continuous process. The relevance of contiguity theory to counseling is remote.

B. Gestalt Theories of Learning

Most associated with Wolfgang Kohler, Max Wertheimer and Kurt Koffka, Gestalt psychology looks at man in a molar rather than in a molecular or reductionist way. Gestalt emphasizes the wholeness of experience. Most attention of gestaltists has been given to perception rather than to learning theory, but a learning theory has been developed. The organism is said to exist in a field. When that field of experience is not in equilibrium, the organism attempts to reduce the disequilibrium by restructuring its experience and perceptions. The principle of an organism's tendency to reduce disequilibrium is called *Pragnanz*. When the field of experience is restored through restructuring, this process is called *insight*. Here learning is a single, goal-oriented process; it is a perceptual restructuring process. It is not a trial and error process, a gradual continuous process or a conditioning process. This theory of learning has many implications in counseling. Should counseling emphasize understanding and insight or should it emphasize small increments in behavioral change outside of counseling? The Gestalt theory of learning is applicable to this dilemma.

C. Purposive Learning Theory (Edward Tolman)

Tolman considered his theory of learning similar to a gestalt model. He differentiated many different types of learning situations (six), having laws specific to each. However, certain generalities held across each situation. Fundamentally, learning was considered a process of organizing perceptual experiences into formations of *expectancies*. Animals and man make predictions at a cognitive level of whether or not their behavior will lead to desired rewards. The organism develops a *cognitive structure* analogous to a field, and it anticipates and predicts what leads to what. Behavior is thus goal directed and purposeful based upon expected outcomes. Drive and need states only emphasize portions of the cognitive structures, but do not act independently to produce learning.

D. S-R Reinforcement Theory (Clark Hull)

Hullian theory is probably the most comprehensive and exhaustive treatment of learning and behavior ever proposed in psychology. His system is an attempt to give a complete system of behavior based upon a series of postulates and corrolaries; it is a highly quantified system as well. Fundamentally, learning is conceived of occurring only under some form of motivational or drive state. It is a drive-reduction theory in that sense. *Habit strength* is the main learning variable, and it is the strength of the bond between a stimulus and a response. The strength of the bond is increased gradually over time. It is a function of the number of trials or exposures to a stimulus situation. Learning is an internal process, but a host of other factors determine whether learning will be manifest in behavior, e.g. the amount of drive and incentive value, the amount of reward, the amount of inhibition, fatigue, etc. Hull's quantified system has been largely replaced, and he is remembered for his historical role in theory building and for his contributions to the understanding of drive and reinforcement. In contrast to the other theories of learning, Hull does not see learning as a cognitive, insightful, single, one-trial event, but as an internal process that occurs continuously. He believed responding is necessary for learning, and motivation and reinforcement are primary to the learning process. Dollard and Miller may be said to derive some of their drive theory in counseling from Hullian influences.

COMMENTARY. Sometimes learning concepts and learning theory have only remote application to counseling theory and practice. A child with a tic, however, may be treated by attaching his arm to an apparatus which administers a small electric shock on a fixed interval schedule whenever a muscle spasm occurs. This is a conditioning procedure as much as it is a psychotherapeutic one. It is based upon some of the principles and theories treated here.

PART **II**

THE GUIDANCE FUNCTION

CHAPTER **4**

THE NATURE OF GUIDANCE

INTRODUCTION. The modern American school is organized around three major functions: administration, instruction, and guidance. As our society has grown technologically and industrially, our students have had to face vastly greater forces within and outside the school which previous generations did not have to confront. The guidance function of the school has grown in parallel fashion with the emerging needs of today's students in order to help them understand and participate in the changing patterns of American culture. For this reason the guidance function of the school is less easily defined than its administrative or instructional counterparts for within its boundaries are contained all of whose unique student needs and concerns which the diversity in American life has fathered.

I. THE DEFINITION OF GUIDANCE

There is by no means any consensus on just what guidance is. It has been defined simply as the *aid or help given by one person to another* or as any *advisory and consultative activity occurring in our schools*. The breadth of these definitions leaves much to be desired for they cause more ambiguity than they clarify. Instead, the definition of guidance has a philosophical dimension, an educational dimension and an activity dimension.

A. Guidance as a Philosophical Entity.

Here guidance is a philosophical concept to foster the maximal development of an individual's unique potentialities.

B. Guidance as an Educational Concept

Translated from philosophy to education, guidance is seen as the provision of a *milieu* in which experiences relating to pupil

55

self-understanding and the understanding of one's own world are afforded.

C. Guidance as an Activity or Service

The implementation of the philosophical and educational dimensions of guidance takes the form of activities or services in the school. In general these guidance services may be seen as the process by which knowledge about the pupil, his patterns of development, his concerns, his choices and his world is gathered as a means of helping him achieve his own goals and individuality. It is an activity or series of services in the school which exist for the students' use.

II. PURPOSES OF GUIDANCE

While there are different schools of thought concerning what guidance is meant to be, some common elements may be drawn.

A. Guidance is concerned with the individual and his needs

B. Guidance exists to enhance personal, social, educational and vocational development

C. Guidance exists to help students profit from instructional experiences and help them develop appropriate decision-making and choice-making skills

III. NEEDS FOR GUIDANCE

The list of problems and needs to which guidance must address itself is too large to be documented in detail. Some overall ideas of the reasons guidance exists, however, is essential.

A. Needs of Special Groups

Certain groups of children have special characteristics requiring specialized attention apart from the normal classroom.

1. *Mentally retarded.*
2. *Emotionally disturbed.*

3. *Physically handicapped.*
4. *Learning disabled.*
5. *Culturally disadvantaged.*
6. *Gifted.*
7. *Perceptually handicapped.*

B. School-related Social Problems

The school must face social problems if it is to be relevant to society at large. The school attempts to address some social problems through the guidance function, not always successfully. It cannot ignore these problems, however.

1. *Illegitimacy and veneral disease.*
2. *School dropouts.*
3. *Juvenile delinquency and crime.*
4. *Racial prejudice.*
5. *Poverty and unemployment.*
6. *Youthful marriages.*
7. *Drug abuse.*
8. *Family disunity, separation, divorce and desertion.*
9. *School failure and underachievement.*

C. Personal Concerns of Pupils

The most frequent personal matters for which guidance is sought are worthy of note in understanding pupil needs for guidance.

1. *Boy-girl relationships, love and marriage.*
2. *Need for self-direction.*
3. *Concern about future vocations.*
4. *Social relationships.*
5. *Responsibility.*
6. *Religion and morality.*
7. *School success and grades.*
8. *Concern for safety and health.*

D. The Family, Community and Economy

The problems of shifting standards in family organization, socio-economic status and class, the varying expectations on children by different social and economic groups all represent forces which cannot be ignored by the school.

IV. GUIDANCE AND PUPIL PERSONNEL SERVICES

Particularly in larger school systems, guidance has been viewed as a sub-function of the comprehensive pupil personnel service. Elsewhere the terms guidance and pupil personnel services have been synonymous. One means of clarifying this issue is to consider all guidance and pupil personnel services as part of the overall *guidance function* leaving the concept of services to be divided between guidance services and other pupil personnel services.

A. Guidance Services

The following four basic school services are commonly developed by the guidance staff.

1. *Appraisal Service.*

The appraisal service concerns the gathering of data about pupils for both individual and institutional needs.

2. *Information Service.*

In order to help students make the appropriate choices and decisions concerning vocational, educational and social opportunities, the information service exists to provide students with the knowledge required in these continuous decision-making areas.

3. *Counseling Service.*

The counseling service is considered the heart of the guidance program, and provides, in both individual and group settings, the opportunity for a relationship to exist in which *personal-social, educational,* and *vocational* needs may be explored.

4. *Placement and Follow-up Services.*

The placement and follow-up services are designed to provide a continuity between in-school and out-of-school educational and employment development for the individual pupil.

B. Other Pupil Personnel Services

Other services offered to the student which may or may not fall under the guidance title, but which are still within the guidance function, are the following pupil personnel activities.

1. *Research and evaluation.*
2. *Psychological services.*
3. *Attendance and accounting services.*
4. *Health, psychiatric and other medical services.*
5. *Social work services.*
6. *Speech and hearing services.*
7. *Remedial reading services.*

V. BASIC PRINCIPLES OF GUIDANCE

There are no explicit scientifically proven absolute principles upon which guidance is founded. Instead, guidance represents a discipline of an applied form which finds its roots in psychology, education, sociology, anthropology, economics and philosophy. It is an interdisciplinary activity. Some of the basic concepts and principles of guidance in education illustrate the wide base upon which guidance rests.

A. **Guidance exists in a democratic context and, therefore, focuses on the individual and his right to choose**

B. **Guidance is developmental and considers the individual in terms of a continuous and sequential development process of growth, maturation and adjustment**

C. **Guidance is an active function which exists as an individualizing element in the school**

D. **Guidance operates between the subjective realities of the individual pupil and the social and external realities which affect his life**

CHAPTER 5

HISTORICAL DEVELOPMENT OF GUIDANCE

INTRODUCTION. The historical development of guidance is illuminating in uncovering the roots which still affect guidance practices in the modern school. In considering the development of guidance, it is possible to look at a number of dimensions: the major *themes* and influences which make up the fabric of the guidance movement, the specific historical *events* which make up guidance chronology, the history of *legislation* which strongly shapes current guidance programming and the *individual personalities* who molded its thinking.

I. MAJOR HISTORICAL INFLUENCES ON GUIDANCE

Rather than consider guidance history in terms of events which often appear as isolated and discrete occurrences, an analysis of the development of guidance by looking at general influences upon it will serve the purpose of an introduction to its chronology.

A. Moral and Philosophical Themes

Growing out of progressive education and the democratic tradition have been certain dominant moral themes governing development.

1. *Freedom of individual to choose.*
2. *The need for a stable moral framework.*
3. *The need to embody normative standards without imposing beliefs on students.*

B. Economic Themes

The impact of automation, changing employment trends and

increasing productivity has greatly influenced changes in guidance practice. Some general principles are resultant.

1. *Guidance is closely linked with educational and economic opportunity by acting as a vehicle through which groups of students can manifest their aspirations.*
2. *Rapidly changing employment trends place increasing emphasis upon earlier and more effective decision-making while in school.*

C. Educational Themes

The growth of educational philosophy and attitudes toward instruction has left guidance with a unique heritage and point of view vis-à-vis education.

1. *Guidance and instruction are interrelated functions.*
2. *Guidance is an individualizing force in instruction.*

D. Mental Measurement Themes

The application of quantitative techniques in increasingly greater number has given guidance important basic concepts.

1. *Reliable, valid and objective evaluations and appraisals of students are essential to guidance technology.*
2. *Tests are well used when they can systematically inform a pupil of his relative standing with other pupils without disregarding his own uniqueness.*
3. *Tests are often economical and efficient devices to observe a certain sample of behavior which otherwise might be too cumbersome to observe.*

E. Mental Hygiene Themes

The mental hygiene movement left with guidance longstanding and fundamental principles.

1. *Emotional needs cannot be ignored in the process of growth, learning and adjustment.*
2. *Unfavorable emotional climates inhibit learning and motivation and hamper personal and social adjustment.*

F. Psychological Themes

It is impossible to list the historical contributions psychology has made to guidance. Instead, it is possible to consider what areas of psychology have had special relevance.

1. *Clinical and diagnostic approaches to pupils.*
2. *Measurement techniques and methods for guidance.*
3. *Learning principles affecting education and adjustment.*
4. *Development, growth and maturation of children.*

G. Social Themes

The impact of sociological forces in shaping thinking about guidance has included some of the following conceptions.

1. *Without knowledge of the student's social milieu and background, an inadequate basis exists for educational, or vocational guidance.*
2. *Guidance practices must be flexible to accomodate changing manpower needs, changing class and peer group composition and changing racial, religious and cultural stereotypes.*

II. IMPORTANT EVENTS IN GUIDANCE

As guidance takes shape from year to year, the interdisciplinary nature of its history becomes clearer. It is equally likely for guidance to take an event in experimental psychology into its own bailiwick as it is for it to claim an event in international politics (Borow, 1964).

A. Precursors of Guidance: 1850–1900

The seeds of guidance were planted in the last half of the nineteenth century.

1. *Wilhelm Wundt established the first psychological laboratory in Leipzig, later followed by G. Stanley Hall in America in 1883.*
2. *Lightner Witmer established the first psychological clinic in 1896.*

3. *Jesse B. Davis began educational-career counseling in Detroit in 1898.*
4. *William Rainey Harper spoke on guidance specialists in universities in 1899 as president of the University of Chicago.*

B. Early Guidance: 1900–1942

1. *In 1907 Eli Weaver published "Choosing a Career."*
2. *Frank Parsons, the father of modern guidance, started the Vocational Bureau of Boston in 1908 and subsequently published "Choosing a Vocation."*
3. *In 1912 Grand Rapids, Michigan began the first citywide guidance department.*
4. *The National Vocational Guidance Association was formed in Grand Rapids in 1913.*
5. *E. L. Thorndike and Robert Yerkes, as part of the war effort, helped develop the Army Alpha and Army Beta tests used for screening military personnel (1917).*
6. *James Burt Miner developed one of the earliest interest questionnaires in 1918.*
7. *A new aspect to vocational guidance appeared in 1925 with the publication of Harry Kitson's "Psychology of Vocational Adjustment."*
8. *In 1927 Clark L. Hull published work on aptitude testing, and E. K. Strong developed the Strong Vocational Interest Blank.*
9. *The National Vocational Guidance Association formed the American Council of Guidance and Personnel Associations in 1934, later to become the current American Personnel and Guidance Association (APGA).*
10. *Robert Hoppock, former NVGA secretary, published "Job Satisfaction," a further insertion of psychology in vocational guidance in 1935.*
11. *L. L. Thurstone, using the new factor analytic techniques, published the "Tests of Primary Mental Abilities" (1938); revised forms are in use today.*
12. *In 1939 the "Dictionary of Occupational Titles" (D.O.T.) first appeared listing 18,000 jobs.*

13. *Carl Rogers radically influenced and reinforced the counseling dimension of guidance with the 1942 publication of "Counseling and Psychotherapy."*

C. World War II to the Present

The impact of the war led to increased measurement and selection activities for processing draftees. This new quantification influenced the appraisal function of modern guidance as well as the research interests of professional guidance specialists.

1. *In 1944 the Army Separation-Classification and Counseling program was established under the War Department for returning veterans.*
2. *The United States Employment Service (USES) developed the General Aptitude Test Battery (GATB) in 1945, an occupational aptitude battery, similar in form to current versions.*
3. *The American Psychological Association established Division 17, Counseling Psychology in 1947.*
4. *The American School Counselor Association (ASCA) was founded in 1952 and became a division of American Personnel and Guidance Association in 1953.*
5. *The Soviet space achievements with Sputnik (1957) lead to major changes in American education, the most immediate of which was the passage of the National Defense Education Act (NDEA) which provided funds for guidance in secondary schools (1958).*
6. *In 1962 APGA published C. Gilbert Wrenn's "Counselor in a Changing World," one of the most influential professional publications of the sixties.*

III. GOVERNMENT SUPPORT OF GUIDANCE

Aid to counseling and guidance activities comes from over seventeen federal acts covering veterans agencies, schools and colleges, rehabilitation programs, mental health centers, etc. The impact of government support and legislation has been great.

A. Early Legislation

Most government support for guidance was of a vocational nature, i.e. the support for vocational education programs and for the establishment of guidance divisions within state departments of education.

1. *1917 Smith-Hughes Act.*
2. *1929 George-Reed Act.*
3. *1934 George-Ellzy Act.*
4. *1938 George-Dean Act.*
5. *1946 George-Barden Act.*

B. Recent Legislation

The volume of federal support has rapidly expanded since the late fifties. Some of the more important legislative acts relating to counseling and guidance are listed.

1. *1958-"National Defense Education Act (NDEA)." One billion dollars was allocated in ten titles to this act. Title five provided over twenty million dollars per year to develop institutes and guidance training and testing programs at both secondary and elementary levels.*
2. *1962-"Manpower Development and Training Act (MDTA)." This act had provisions to include guidance services to persons who were economically displaced or to those persons who were under-employed.*
3. *1964-"Economic Opportunity Act." EOA established the Job Corps, Vista and Head Start programs, and these activities indirectly influenced the continued development and expansion of guidance activities.*
4. *1965-"Elementary-Secondary Education Act (ESEA)." This act is composed of six titles and supports aid to educationally deprived children, educational research and training and funds for supplemental educational services, e.g. remedial instruction, counseling, social work, etc.*

IV. PERSONALITIES INFLUENCING GUIDANCE DEVELOPMENT

Certain persons within and outside counseling and guidance

have contributed to guidance development and have had tremendous influence and impact on its theory and practice. Some of these personalities are listed.

A. Frank Parsons

As earlier indicated Parsons began vocational guidance in Boston. It is for this reason that Parsons is referred to as the father of vocational guidance. His technique was to match man requirements with job requirements and this process became an historical tradition in vocational guidance. It was a precursor to the trait-factor approach.

B. E. G. Williamson

Largely expanding and adding to the model of Parsons, Williamson applied the trait-factor, matching techniques to counseling and personality. This approach had great impact at the secondary school and college level.

C. Donald G. Paterson

Paterson's work is particularly recognized in vocational counseling, the organization of personnel services and the development of diagnostic and appraisal devices.

D. Carl Rogers

The client-centered therapy of Rogers was uniquely compatible with the growth of guidance, and through its emphasis on the integrity and worth of each individual, helped to spur a more democratic philosophy within guidance. He is also known for the objectification of counseling and psychotherapy by the systematic use of tape recordings of sessions for research and training of counselors.

E. C. Gilbert Wrenn

Wrenn has served as the editor of the *Journal of Counseling Psychology,* acted as a consultant with the Department of Labor and Office of Education and has written prolifically in guidance for a long time. Historically, he is viewed as a consolidating and unifying influence on guidance development.

F. James A. Conant

As one of the most influential educators in America, Conant's studies of our schools and his recommendations to superintendents for improved guidance practices has helped the development and professionalization of school counseling.

G. Freud, Piaget, and Skinner

Freud's psychoanalytic theory and methods, as well as Piaget's work in the development of children's conceptual abilities, have provided foundations upon which developmental guidance has grown, i.e. guidance which is seen as a continuous process rather than a one step experience occurring at the end of high school. Skinner's work in reinforcement theory has spurred the creation of whole new ways of looking at and dealing with behavior problems in schools, individualizing instruction and devising techniques of developing curricular materials. Few counselors are not acquainted with the works of these men.

V. CONTEMPORARY ORGANIZATION OF COUNSELING PSYCHOLOGY AND GUIDANCE

The development of the professional institutions of counseling and guidance has occurred continuously since the beginning of the National Vocational Guidance Association in Grand Rapids, Michigan in 1913. Currently most professionals who are identified with the broad area of counseling psychology and guidance are members of two parent professional organizations each with respective subdivisions. Most of the professional journals are published in association with these subdivisions.

A. American Psychological Association (APA)

This sprawling, professional organization of psychologists has numerous divisions covering the major areas of specialization in psychology from clinical to physiological psychology. *Division 17* is called the Division of Counseling Psychology and publishes the *Journal of Counseling Psychology* six times per year. This division has the most immediate relevance to counseling and guidance; however, APA also publishes other journals frequently used by members of the counseling profession.

1. *American Psychologist.*
2. *Contemporary Psychology.*
3. *Journal of Abnormal Psychology.*
4. *Journal of Applied Psychology.*
5. *Journal of Comparative and Physiological Psychology.*
6. *Journal of Consulting Psychology.*
7. *Journal of Educational Psychology.*
8. *Journal of Experimental Psychology.*
9. *Journal of Personality and Social Psychology.*
10. *Psychological Abstracts.*
11. *Psychological Bulletin.*
12. *Psychological Review.*

B.   American Personnel and Guidance

APGA was formed in 1951 and has steadily grown. Currently, it has eight subdivisions. APGA, the parent organization, publishes its own journal, *The Personnel and Guidance Journal.* Subdivisions of the organization and journals sponsored by each are listed.

1. *National Employment Counselors Association (NECA); "Journal of Employment Counseling."*
2. *National Vocational Guidance Association (NVGA); "Vocational Guidance Quarterly."*
3. *American College Personnel Association (ACPA); "Journal of College Student Personnel."*
4. *Association for Counselor Education and Supervision; "Counselor Education and Supervision" (Journal of).*
5. *Student Personnel Association for Teacher Education (SPATE); "SPATE Journal."*
6. *American School Counselor Association (ASCA): the "School Counselor." This is the largest of the subdivisions of APGA.*
7. *American Rehabilitation Counseling Association (ARCA); "Rehabilitation Counseling Bulletin."*
8. *Association for Measurement and Evaluation (AMEG); "Measurement and Evaluation in Guidance."*

C. Other Journals

There are other relevant publications for counselors not covered by these two professional organizations.

1. *Review of Educational Research.*
2. *Journal of Clinical Psychology.*
3. *Psychotherapy: Theory, Research and Practice.*
4. *Educational and Psychological Measurement.*
5. *Journal of Humanistic Psychology.*

COMMENTARY: Where guidance was one affected by the emphasis upon mental measurement and placement, as in World War II classification efforts, it is today responding to existentialist thought. Where it was once an activity only for the special student, increasingly it is an activity that all students have a right to. Where it was once nondirective, it is today operant and experimental. And where it once functioned coercively to enforce society's standards at all levels in the school, it is now often an opportunity to escape from the tyranny of such coercion to form one's own values and approach to life in the protected atmosphere of a counseling relationship. In short, guidance development is dynamic and, to a remarkable degree, fluid. There are, of course, trends which are recognizable, and there are methods of making probabilistic predictions of what guidance might be five years hence. These speculations belong to a more detailed study of guidance history than is given here. One conclusion, however, which deserves mention is that change is occurring, and each year it occurs somewhat faster!

CHAPTER 6

PHILOSOPHY AND THEORY
OF GUIDANCE

INTRODUCTION. It seems hard to imagine that when a student is administered a particular personality test through the guidance program, this activity is related to the overall philosophical approach taken by the guidance staff. Indeed, many of the activities engaged in by guidance personnel are not worked out in terms of philosophy or theory. In the main, however, guidance begins with a *philosophy* which leads to the acceptance of a particular *theoretical model*. From such a model the basis for *policy, planning,* and the inevitable *program structure* is derived. A review of the philosophical nature of guidance and the variety of theoretical models currently in the literature, therefore, is a necessary precursor to the understanding of how guidance is organized, administered and, perhaps, why it does what it does.

I. THE DIMENSIONS OF PHILOSOPHY

A particular philosophical system must relate to the major dimensions of philosophical thought, though it may emphasize one dimension over another.

A. Metaphysics

A philosophical system may be viewed in terms of its own *theory of reality,* and its emphasis on the nature of man, the nature of existence, etc.

B. Epistemology

As guidance concerns education, so too does a guidance model have to come to terms with the *nature of knowledge* and how man knows.

C. Axiology

It is often said in guidance that each counselor maintains his own *theory of values* which guide his practice. In this way the counselor assumes an axiological position.

D. Logic

Some models assert that only through observation and experimentation can one come to know the basic governing principles in guidance (*inductive* logic). Others assert that guidance behavior must be dictated by an overall conceptualization, not by isolated and discrete procedures (*deductive* logic). Every model must take a logical system, whatever the mode of approach.

II. SYSTEMS OF PHILOSOPHY

Five major philosophical systems exist into which theories of guidance may fall.

A. Rationalism

The rational approach is one emphasizing the cultivation of reason and the notion that the nature or essence of reality is a constellation of rational principles.

B. Idealism

Like the rationalist, the idealist sees reality in abstract rather than concrete terms. Emphasis here, however, is given more to the spiritual nature of man than in rationalism.

C. Realism

The realist assumes the independent existence of external reality and thereby sees knowledge as an objective process of *disclosure* to the knower.

D. Experimentalism

To the experimentalist, or *pragmatist,* knowledge is not a disclosure to a passive recipient, but an interaction between knower and known. Learning comes through doing. Nothing exists independently, but all elements of reality have a mutual interrelatedness.

E.   Existentialism

The existentialist approach is the most subjective system mentioned. It stresses man's tentativeness in the world, his freedom to be and the legitimacy of his own uniqueness.

III.   PHILOSOPHY AND GUIDANCE

The relationship between specific philosophical systems and guidance approaches is not entirely clear. One guidance model may have elements of rationalism in terms of its view of education but aspects of existentialism in terms of its view of the individual in counseling. One may take the view, however, that inasmuch as guidance and counseling rest upon a scientific base, specifically psychology, the experimentalist position is fundamental.

IV.   MODELS FOR GUIDANCE

Guidance models have evolved. They follow an historical continuum of development. Moreover, in each there is a philosophical thread and an attitude about man (Schertzer & Stone, 1966).

A.   Directive Guidance

The directive approach in guidance is most closely associated with the *Parsonian* model which began at the Vocational Bureau of Boston in 1908. The guidance process is seen as mentor or specialist oriented in which specific prescriptions are given for specific needs at discrete points in time. Guidance here is a one step intervention process. The procedures employed usually entail an *individual analysis* of a student's capabilities, a *job analysis* of needed skills, and a *synthesis* of the two sets of analyses which result in specific prescriptive recommendations.

1. *Advantages.*

The advantages of this rational-directive approach lie in the economy provided to the school in conceptualizing guidance activities as single-operation functions. Such an approach tends to appeal to the pragmatic American spirit, and it is for this reason that the model characterized so much of guidance in its early years.

2. *Disadvantages*.

Such a model makes the assumption that the student cannot learn about himself and understand himself to a significant degree, thus requiring a mentor who, through the application of objective and formal information gathering instruments, makes recommendations and plans for the pupil.

B. Educative Guidance

During the 1930s the notion that guidance is education and education is guidance took popular form. No longer were instruction and guidance seen as two of the school's functions, but that both were identical in aim.

1. *Advantages*.

This guidance strategy helped to enlarge the focus of guidance, incorporate more activities and helped focus the efforts of schools more on students than subjects.

2. *Disadvantages*.

The model may assume guidance is not only continuous but is to be monolithically applied to all pupils regardless of their individual capacities and desire to enter into such programs.

C. Adjustive and Distributive Guidance

Most closely associated with *William Proctor* in the 1920s, guidance was conceived as two processes: helping students and society effect an appropriate *distribution* of persons in educational and vocational positions, and helping students *adjust* to and integrate their own knowledge of themselves and the world about them. The adjustive principle takes on the personal-social dimension, while the distributive principle chiefly concerns the educational-vocational dimension.

1. *Advantages*.

The advantage of the model lies in its emphasis upon the

personal-social dimension, and the concept of students making their own choices in the adjustment process.

2. *Disadvantages.*

The adjustive mode of guidance may easily take on a reactive form, i.e. one which serves only those students in need of special help during crises. It therefore becomes a piecemeal operation.

D. Clinical Guidance

The clinical guidance model is an outgrowth of directive guidance. It derives primarily from the influence of the mental measurement movement and stands as a reaction to the oftentimes unreliable and mediocre techniques found in many guidance approaches. The clinical model attempts to bring specialists into the guidance program, each bringing with him definitive and orderly procedures and techniques for his particular function. Its emphasis is on the roles each participant takes in bringing an interdisciplinary team together in dealing with the individual pupil comprehensively. *Donald Paterson* and *E.G. Williamson* are most linked to this heavily rational approach.

1. *Advantages.*

The approach has the advantage of economy and efficiency to the school as well as the increased competency offered to improve the quality of the guidance program.

2. *Disadvantages.*

The emphasis upon formal and external techniques may impede other means of information gathering, or interfere with the relationship between counselor and client by interpolating impersonal instrumentation between them.

E. Eclectic Guidance

The eclectic approach is one taking the view that many methods and techniques are currently available to the guidance worker, irrespective of the philosophical foundations upon which they may rest. Guidance is seen as a process made up of two major functions: *adjustment* of the individual to choice-making educational opportunities, etc., and *appraisal* of the pupil to aid in this overall process. The aim of guidance is to know and help the individual; any techniques and approaches which are valuable are to be used by the eclectic practitioner for this aim. *Ruth Strang* is most associated with this view.

1. *Advantages.*

The primary advantage of the eclectic approach is the freedom it gives the professional to utilize and explore various methods and techniques.

2. *Disadvantages.*

An eclectic approach may lead to mediocrity by not being guided by a consistent philosophy.

F.   Developmental Guidance

Developmental guidance is of a more contemporary nature than previously mentioned approaches. It posits that the goal of guidance is the achievement of individual adequacy and effectiveness through self knowledge and understanding. This principle is manifested in the notion that a team effort in the school (teachers, counselors, administrators) is best geared to this general aim. Moreover, the aim of guidance must be seen as a continuous process at all levels of education, not a one step crisis intervention technique. *Gail Farwell* is most typically associated with this view (Peters & Farwell, 1967).

1. *Advantages.*

The notion that young and old alike have special needs and adjustment difficulties at all levels of school involvement and that guidance is relevant to the individual at all points in his development is the major asset of this approach.

2. *Disadvantages.*

The approach is impractical. Resources do not exist in such abundance to provide services to all students at all levels. Secondly, not all teachers and administrators accept the basic aim of the developmental model, and are not necessarily fully competent to carry it out if they do.

G. Teleological Guidance

David Tiedeman's 1962 proposal that guidance assume a teleological or purposeful-action model is a novel model for contemporary guidance. The approach sees guidance in terms of its relationship to choice and decision-making. The school produces discontinuities for the pupil. Guidance exists to help the individual purposefully choose those actions which will reduce those discontinuities.

1. *Advantages.*

Fundamentally, conceiving of guidance as a process of choice through purposeful action adds much to the guidance movement. While we know students make choices because of their past background and present experiences, this model asserts that students will make more effective decisions about the future if they have experience in decision making itself. Regardless of the alternatives available to each child, Tiedeman's model assumes that in *any* choice situation there is an ideal model and process to follow. The more experience one has with it, the more effective his decisions will be in the future.

2. *Disadvantages.*

The model is highly experimental and few professional counselors are in the position of programming it into a school with competence.

H. Reconstructive Guidance

It is said in some quarters that guidance exists to support and induce the movement of students into the value systems of the middle class. *Shoben* contends that guidance exists to reinforce individuality and autonomy, not traditionalist conformity. Edward Shoben's approach places guidance as the key school element which helps the student express his distinctiveness and find his own unique value system. To program such an aim in the school entails a massive reconstruction of the whole school effort.

1. *Advantages.*

The model is consonant with the majority belief that guidance must help facilitate individuality.

2. *Disadvantages.*

In view of the current structure of educational systems, the model would appear somewhat unrealistic in trying to reconstruct the schools in this fashion.

COMMENTARY: There is no clear line from philosophy to guidance. Ideally one's behavior is based on sound theory, but realistically a guidance specialist behaves in ways with children which are unrelated to his metaphysics or theory of epistemology. If the student has difficulty relating philosophical types with specific guidance models, it is likely that such confusion is well founded.

CHAPTER 7

GUIDANCE RELATIONSHIPS

INTRODUCTION. Like any other applied discipline, guidance is anchored in many contexts. Reciprocal interests and responsibilities exist between guidance and the teacher, guidance and curriculum, guidance and the administrative functions of the school, and between guidance and the community. An awareness of these patterns of responsibility helps the guidance worker to find his roots as well as his resources.

I. GUIDANCE AND THE TEACHER

The major function of guidance is an individualizing or personalizing of the school experience. The major responsibility and function of the teacher is in facilitating the acquisition of knowledge and skills. In most schools the agent in direct contact with the student most of the time is the teacher. The teacher cannot be ignored or by-passed by a guidance program no matter how resourceful and specialized it may be, for without the aid of the teacher, the guidance function is paralyzed. On the other hand, the teacher is not primarily a guidance specialist and cannot be expected to carry out major guidance responsibilities.

A. The Teacher and Counseling

The teacher often has private and personal conferences with students. Some overlap between this activity and counseling must generally occur. A teacher who is properly oriented to counseling and who is sensitive to the needs of pupils can both profit from such private conferences and help the pupil toward greater self-understanding, as well as to know where the line between counseling and teacher conferences is drawn, such that the teacher knows how and when to recommend the student to counseling. In this sense the teacher is a major resource and referral person for the counselor.

B. The Teacher and Other Guidance Functions

Through the role of a discussion leader or coordinator of voluntary discussion and study groups, the teacher may enhance those guidance activities concerned with *occupational, social* and *educational information exploration, educational-vocational planning, school orientation and articulation,* and *job placement.* The teacher also plays an important role as a consultant in parent conferences with the guidance staff.

II. GUIDANCE AND THE CURRICULUM

The curriculum is the focal point of instruction and is implemented through the teacher. What differentiates curriculum from guidance is that guidance takes on an individual form while curricular-instructional activities are group oriented. The relationship, however, is not so easily distinguished and separated. The developments toward *individualized instruction* through diagnostic, prescriptive and remedial teaching methodologies have come to recognize the necessity of tailoring curriculum to the individual needs, interests, and inadequacies of pupils. In this capacity the relationship between the testing functions of guidance and the individual appraisal service share a close relationship to curriculum planning and development. Moreover, the curriculum stands as a major resource for the guidance worker in implementing many of the guidance activities for specific students.

III. GUIDANCE AND ADMINISTRATION

The strength of a guidance program is heavily weighted with the interest taken by the school administration. The interests of administrators toward guidance usually involves the provision of services and care to pupils and the evaluation of guidance and other school services through research. Guidance looks to administration for leadership in forming an effective and integrated guidance program, particularly as this concerns appropriate allocation and utilization of personnel and resources. Where guidance personnel fail to articulate their professional competencies and properly orient administrators to guidance, misconceptions and distortions of the role of counselors and other guidance specialists can result. A trained counselor who spends the majority of his time in pupil accounting, discipline and testing, with only a minor portion of his time alloted to counseling, has failed to muster the administrative support required to effectively implement his own competencies.

IV. GUIDANCE AND THE COMMUNITY

The guidance worker must understand the community in which he works. An entirely college-bound student population needs fewer vocational activities than a less privileged community. The guidance program, therefore, varies in direct relation to community needs. In general the guidance function is related to the community in two capacities.

A. Articulation

Because guidance needs the community for such reasons as providing summer and in-school educational-vocational work experiences, it must articulate its goals and programs in the community. The degree to which guidance can avail itself of community resources, and vice versa, depends largely on the quality of articulation given.

B. Resources and Referral

Any single community has more resources for guidance than is generally known. Parents alone, through their willingness and interest in guidance, play a major role in the implementation of recommendations. The vast array of employers, vocational training programs and opportunities, community mental health and social services, state professional societies, etc., are all potential resources the guidance specialists may use for referral of students having particular needs. The use of these resources depends first upon the awareness of the guidance worker and secondly upon how he has articulated his role and image to the community.

V. GUIDANCE AND THE STUDENT

When organizing for guidance, the particular extensity of the curriculum must be examined; the resources and provisions of the administration must be studied; the character and needs of the community must be considered. The major component of guidance policy and program, however, must inevitably be dictated by the student. In this sense, guidance must be viewed as an active force which assesses those student needs which must be met and engages the administration, curriculum, teacher and community in making a commitment to the student and providing the services which will meet his needs.

CHAPTER **8**

ORGANIZATION AND ADMINISTRATION OF GUIDANCE

INTRODUCTION. Some schools have no provisions for guidance services and employ no counselors. Other schools are incorporated into metropolitan school systems employing thousands of teachers, administrators and guidance personnel. Within these two extremes, the organizational patterns of guidance and their administrations are found.

I. TRADITIONAL ORGANIZATIONAL PATTERNS

Every school has some form of operational structure and formal organization with specific designations of authority and responsibility. The theory of administration gives four basic types of operational structure. (Schertzer and Stone, 1966).

A. Line-staff Organization

Line structure involves the *distribution of authority* from highest to lowest levels. Staff organization involves the *distribution of functions* to be performed. Line personnel take responsibility and authority for decisions and commands while staff personnel execute those decisions within their particular functional area.

B. Scalar Organization

A hierarchy of duties (functions) and degree of authority in decision making is called scalar organization. A principle and a school psychologist, for example, may have the same decision-making power granted to them under the superintendent of schools, but they have separate functions under him.

C. Spatial Organization

The spatial character of organization concerns the location or geography of particular services. This form of operation is concerned chiefly with *centralization-decentralization dimension.*

D. Radial Organization

A sometimes more democratic form of organization is the *hub* concept in which the executive takes the center position and all other functions or services have equal authority in a circle around him. Commands in this way may be reduced and greater emphasis placed upon consensus and recommendations to the executive.

II. OTHER ORGANIZATIONAL CONCEPTS

There are other ways of thinking about the organization of guidance. Glanz (1964) has cited four other types of guidance organization. These organizational schemes are determined by the philosophy and purpose of the guidance program, the size of the school, the level of professional activity, etc.

A. Centralized Specialism

Often using a pupil personnel model, the centralization of various specialists, e.g. social workers, counselors and school psychologists, in one area provides for the placing of highly qualified specialists together in a coordinated team approach to pupil problems.

B. Decentralized Generalism

In this approach specialists are avoided and guidance filters into all classrooms through the teacher and other administrative and instructional staff. Guidance is a function assumed by all school personnel to some extent.

C. Curricular Counseling and Guidance

Group guidance and other programming of guidance through course units, e.g. occupations classes, nested within the curriculum characterize this approach.

D. Human Relations and Group Work

This system is less organizational than philosophical inasmuch as it implies a broad mental health approach in the school rather than a specific designation of personnel to implement it. Organizationally this model would probably be found between centralized specialism and decentralized generalism.

III. CENTRALIZATION VERSUS DECENTRALIZATION OF GUIDANCE

The growth of any profession or service usually brings with it a tendency toward consolidation and centralization. Guidance, not unlike other movements, has expressed its growing pains in a similar way as it moves from a single part time guidance worker in an isolated school to a coordinated, centralized division of pupil personnel services operating from the office of the superintendent at its downtown headquarters. Advantages and disadvantages alike are found with both centralized and decentralized organizations.

A. Advantages and Disadvantages of Centralization

Centralized organization is more efficient in avoiding duplicated efforts, and has the advantage of maintaining a consistent philosophy and orientation through facilitated communication in a central location. It suffers, however, by taking a guidance role away from the teacher, deemphasizing her responsibility in the whole effort toward the child and promoting a detachment of the guidance staff from the school milieu.

B. Advantages and Disadvantages of Decentralization

A decentralized plan allows for continuity in communication and effort between staff, teacher and student-in-situation. More concern is given to the total learning environment of the child. On the other hand, a decentralized plan usually means the guidance staff have widely discrepant backgrounds and approaches, depend too heavily on the teacher for providing services and do not function in a coordinated or meaningful way so that teachers, students, parents and other non guidance persons really know what guidance is or does.

IV. ROLES AND RESPONSIBILITIES
IN THE ORGANIZATIONAL SCHEME

Many professionals participate in guidance activities. The actual administrators, their roles, responsibilities and titles almost wholly depend upon the specific school situation in which they function. In general, however, we may look at an ideal model of a guidance operation in a very large school system in order to understand most of the types and kinds of personnel involved in guidance administration. The model begins at the top of executive authority and proceeds to the specific personnel dealing with the child.

A. Board of Education

The school board represents local control of education, and is responsible only to the state legislature. Typically, the school board engages in the following types of behavior:

1. *Establishes schools and buys school property.*
2. *Levies taxes and establishes spending policies.*
3. *Employs the superintendent of schools.*
4. *Establishes school policies and standards through the superintendent.*

B. Superintendents

The superintendent is the liaison between the community and the school establishment. His relationship to guidance is crucial, for he sets the pace, tone and character of guidance services and interprets these to the community and the board of education as he does for other school services. The quality of guidance services is directly related to the initiative and leadership taken by the superintendent.

C. The Guidance Council or Committee

Also called the *pupil personnel services council,* the guidance committee is an advisory board directly concerned with district-wide guidance programming. It helps coordinate and establish guidance policy, conducts evaluations of the programs and advises the director of guidance on staff recommendations, budget, resources, etc. The members of this committee may be teachers, counselors, principals, superintendents or others depending upon the specific district operation. The committee generally does not have great executive authority, but serves in an advisory capacity. Furthermore, it may not necessarily be a permanent body.

D. Director of Pupil Personnel Services

Also called the director of guidance or the director of special services, the director of pupil personnel services is solely responsible to the superintendent of schools, typically a line relationship. His relationship is usually parallel or equivalent to the director of instruction and the director of business or administrative services. The responsibilities of the director are:

1. *General supervision and coordination of guidance services.*
2. *Coordination of guidance with instructional services.*
3. *Professional supervision of counselors.*
4. *Evaluation and articulation of guidance services.*
5. *Responsibility for all special services, implementing regulatory laws, etc.*

E. Principals and Assistant Principals

The building principals are usually *administratively* responsible for guidance staff though not *professionally* responsible for them. Their main relationships with guidance concern scheduling, coordination of resources and planning with other school services and consultative duties with teachers and counselors. The assistant principals often are required to implement attendance laws, schedule classes, take some responsibility for group guidance activities and assume responsibility for discipline.

F. Specialists in the Guidance Program

The pluralistic nature of guidance must be recognized. Some schools have needs and resources for some specialists more than others. There is great variety in the types of specialists employed part or full time in any given guidance program. Some of the major specialists, however, are worthy of mention.

1. *School Psychologists.*

The major function of the school psychologist is psycho-educational diagnosis and remediation. This includes testing and appraisal of the mentally retarded and emotionally disturbed, recommendations for placements in special classes, etc.

2. *School Social Workers.*

Sometimes referred to as a *visiting teacher,* the school social worker is involved in case work services with pupils and their families, referral of children and parents to special community agencies and provision of consultative services to other guidance specialists working with a child.

3. *School Nurse.*

The school nurse assists in the routine physical examinations required by state law, conducts annual hearing and vision tests, gives emergency first aid, maintains health records and participates in the general prevention and control of illness in the school.

4. *Other Medical Personnel.*

School psychiatrists, physicians, pediatricians, and the like serve as medical consultants to special education programs, to the teacher, the administration and other guidance staff.

5. *Speech and Hearing Therapist.*

The speech and hearing therapist usually conducts screening of speech, voice and language behavior, diagnoses the types of communication disorders and provides group and individual speech and hearing therapy.

6. *Reading Specialists.*

The reading specialist functions to help establish a sound reading program as well as a sound remedial reading program, helps in the diagnosis of reading disability and acts as a resource person in providing remedial materials for children.

7. *School Counselors.*

The school counselor assists in the development of the guidance program, conducts individual and group counseling, is involved with pupil appraisal, educational and occupational planning and placement, consults with parents and other guidance staff and engages in research. The role of the school counselor is developed in greater detail elsewhere.

8. *Other Related Specialists.*

Some teachers have an especially close affinity with the guidance operation. Teachers of the perceptually handicapped, learning disabled, mentally retarded, emotionally disturbed, as well as remedial reading teachers, all work closely with guidance in implementing different aspects of the recommendations prepared for particular special children.

CHAPTER 9

THE INFORMATION SERVICE

INTRODUCTION. The information service usually administered by the guidance staff is a cooperative enterprise between teachers, administrators and counselors to provide the resources and facilities to satisfy the informational needs of students as well as to facilitate pupil awareness of available information and its appropriate and effective utilization.

I. PURPOSES AND OBJECTIVES OF THE INFORMATION SERVICE

Most informational services have typically confined themselves to the secondary level. Elementary school information exploration is gathering increasing attention, and the differences between elementary and secondary level information services is striking in terms of basic purposes and objectives. A special chapter is devoted to the guidance function at the elementary level at the end of this text. The general objectives and characteristics of the information service at the secondary level will be treated here.

A. Broad Understanding

One purpose of the informational services provided by the school is to promote a wide awareness of the fields of work and occupation.

B. Depth Exploration

The information service should be designed to give the interested and motivated student adequate resources and facilities to fully explore his particular area of interest.

C. Awareness of Alternatives

The student should become appraised of all the educational and occupational possibilities open to him.

D. Planning

The information service is the fundamental resource in the school for students to thoroughly explore information in order to plan educational and vocational careers.

E. Personalizing Information

Individuals with special needs require special types of information. In many ways all students need an individualized and tailored encounter with educational, social and occupational information. One purpose, then, of the information service is to create this individualizing quality in the service rather than to lump all informational materials together blindly.

II. TYPES OF INFORMATION

There are three basic types of information, occupational, educational and social, each having a specific definition and characterization.

A. Occupational Information

Occupational information is useful and accurate data about employment positions and occupations including information on entrance requirements, duties, remuneration, advancement, conditions of work, needs for services and resources for further investigation.

B. Educational Information

Adequate educational information is any useful and accurate data concerning all types of educational and training possibilities, both present and future, which include statements on requirements, characteristics of student life and activities, as well as descriptions of curricular offerings.

C. Social Information

Personal-social information is accurate and useful data on the factors and influences on the human physical and social environment which bear on personal adjustment and interpersonal relations.

III. VARIETIES OF INFORMATIONAL MATERIALS

Establishing an information center or library is a task undertaken by the guidance staff with considerable caution. The varieties of information alone are so large that careful selection of appropriate types is essential. A broad picture of the types of materials used is given here.

A. Occupational Information

Occupational information is the most prolific area of information and the one requiring the most attention by the staff in selection, filing and fluid utilization.

1. *Career Fiction and Biography.*

Used primarily at the elementary and junior high level, these texts are frequently general, high-interest publications dramatized to elicit greater awareness and understanding of particular occupational roles.

2. *Job Descriptions.*

A brief, concise statement about qualifications, duties and other relevant matters concerning employment is called a job description.

3. *Occupational Descriptions.*

This is a comprehensive description of an occupation in and across a number of industries and establishments.

4. *Occupational Brief.*

Probably the most widely used type of occupational material, the brief is a description of the background of an occupation, entrance requirements, roles, responsibilities, rewards, hours and methods of entrance. The brief is usually from 3,000 to 5,000 words.

5. *Occupational Monographs.*

Ranging from 6,000 to 10,000 words, the monograph is longer and more detailed, but more cumbersome to prepare, evaluate and up-date. It gives extensive coverage to all phases of an occupation.

6. *Job Series.*

A job series is usually a document covering a broad area of work, and all job opportunities in the field.

7. *Community Survey.*

This is a highly comprehensive report on local occupations and how they are distributed.

8. *Dictionary of Occupational Titles (D.O.T.).*

Published by the United States Employment Service (USES), the D.O.T. codes and classifies occupations in terms of the broad categories of work in which the job is found and in terms of the level of worker functions involved.

B. Educational Information

The major educational information documents generally follow a more uniform format.

1. *College Catalogs.*

The college catalog typically contains information on admission, housing, tuition, scholarships, loans and fees, as well as curricular requirements and offerings.

2. *Educational Directories.*

The college directory is designed to provide an index to various types of colleges and universities in terms of certain limited criteria: admissions, accreditation, fees, awards, degree offerings, etc. Some of the more prominent directories are noteworthy.

a. *Lovejoy's College Guide.*
b. *Vocational Training Directory of the United States.*
c. *Directory of Technical Institute Courses.*

3. *Financial Aid Information.*

The increasing variety of scholarship and loan programs has resulted in the publication of numerous directories of financial aid from local, private, institutional and national sources.

4. *Examination Directories and Study Guides.*

In order to help students to become aware of national testing programs and national and regional scholarship examinations, numerous texts, directories and study guides have been produced for this purpose.

C. Social Information

Some commercial organizations have made available useable books, kits and topic-oriented personal-social materials for the information library. This material, however, is small in comparison with the quantities of occupational and educational information in circulation.

1. *Level or Age-Specific Material.*

Social information is correlated with development. There are primary, elementary, junior high school, senior high school and adult levels of social information.

2. *Topic Specific.*

Social materials may be found on most topics e.g. cheating, growing up, timidity, menstruation, drugs, etc. Selecting appropriate topics for appropriate age level, however, becomes necessary.

IV. SELECTION AND EVALUATION OF INFORMATION

It cannot be overemphasized that definite criteria must be followed in evaluating and selecting appropriate materials for the information service. Some guidelines may be general to all information, others specific to the various types of information to be used.

A. General Screening Guidelines

1. *Is the material published by a reputable publisher?*
2. *Is the author listed and qualified?*
3. *Is the material objective or does it attempt to present only one point of view? Occupational recruitment literature often fails this test.*
4. *Is the material current?*
5. *Is the material readable at the levels intended?*
6. *Is the material appealing and well illustrated?*

B. Specific Evaluative Criteria

Occupational and educational information have received rigorous examination by guidance professionals and numerous criteria for adequate information have evolved from this effort.

1. *Occupational Information.*
   a. *The purpose of the information should be clear.*
   b. *The information should be appropriate* and geared to age, grade and socio-economic level.
   c. *The material should be relevant* to all groups in our society.
   d. *The material should be unbiased and representative.*
   e. *The material should include information on satisfactions for the worker as well as possible demands.*
   f. *The content of the occupational information should include the history and definition of the occupation, the nature of the work, entrance requirements and methods, advancement opportunities, employment outlook, earnings, conditions of work, psycho-social factors and sources of more information.*

2. *Educational Information.*

The criteria for evaluation of educational information is somewhat more general.
   a. *Author and publisher should be listed.*
   b. *Publications should be recent.*
   c. *The document should be authentic.*
   d. *The material should be suitable in terms of cost, style, readability, completeness and format.*

V. THE INFORMATION SERVICE LIBRARY

Organizing the information service library is one function of the guidance staff. The process consists of *selecting the personnel* to organize and manage the library, *finding suitable locations* for the materials and equipment, *selecting the materials* according to local needs and available resources, *developing a filing plan* which is efficiently and easily used by students and providing for *systematic review* of the center, its relevance, contemporaneousness and its improvement. Some basic minimum core of materials has been found essential to a meaningful information center (Noris, Zeran & Hatch, 1966).

A. Basic Elements for the Library: Occupational Materials

1. *Occupational Outlook Handbook.*
2. *Occupational Outlook Quarterly.*
3. *National Vocational Guidance Association (VGA) Bibliography of Current Occupational Literature.*
4. *The Vocational Guidance Quarterly.*
5. *Guide to Career Information and Occupational Literature: An Annotated Bibliography.*
6. *A Monthly Annotated Bibliography e.g. Occupational Index or Counselor Information Service.*
7. *Dictionary of Occupational Titles, Vols. 1 and 2.*
8. *Standard Industrial Classification Manual.*

B. Basic Elements for the Library: Educational Materials

1. *Catalogs from state institutions: noncollege and college.*
2. *A directory of colleges and universities nationwide.*
3. *A vocational school directory.*
4. *A directory of correspondence and home study schools.*
5. *A directory of scholarship and financial aid information.*
6. *Materials on how to study, selecting a college, etc.*

VI. USING INFORMATION

Information exploration frequently takes place in a number of ways. Students may come to the library to explore educational and vocational information individually. They may wish to discuss their career plans and opportunities in individual counseling, or they may wish to participate or organize group activities around information exploration. Rather than waiting for self-seeking student exploration, however, the guidance staff may actively attempt to facilitate information exploration.

A. Individual Information Exploration

There is a belief that the counseling process is not the most appropriate way for the individual to explore educational and occupational information in that it places the counselor in an authoritarian role or a data oriented one. Students, however, do seek out the counselor for assistance in career planning, and at many points in the counseling process, information enters the counselor-client interaction. Some guidelines for the discussion of occupational information in counseling have been suggested.

1. *Client Need.*

Client need should determine whether information enters the counseling relationship and when it should be explored.

2. *Non-manipulative.*

Information is not fed to the client nor is it used in any persuasive or manipulative way. Instead, the focus of the counseling relationship is to seek the client's internalization or subjective reaction to the information.

3. *Decision-making and Feedback.*

Information exploration, along with other devices, e.g. aptitude tests, may be used to facilitate client planning, generate occupational and educational alternatives, simulate various points of the decision making process, provide feedback for the client along this exploration process, etc.

4. *Client Readiness and Occupational Maturity.*

Occupations often represent clients' implementations of their self-concepts. To some extent what a person *wishes to become* in the future is a fantasy and, at various ages in the client's life, it is always to some degree realistic and to another degree unrealistic. Similarly, in a counseling relationship the client exhibits a certain degree of occupational maturity and a readiness for a certain type of information. Here the counselor's sensitivity to these factors may determine the successful selection and use of information.

B. Group Information Exploration

Most efficient use of information can be provided at the group level if properly programmed and managed.

1. *Guidance Courses.*

Most frequently used at the entry level of secondary school, the guidance course can be organized according to a general approach in which the broad outlines of educational and vocational planning are given, or as a special unit having a more defined purpose. Guidance courses have not met with distinguishing success because materials were inadequate, staff poorly trained and pupil motivation variable.

2. *Occupations Courses.*

Occupations courses may be effectively used with vocationally motivated students, particularly when following a well-defined course outline which is relevant to student concerns. Special techniques of writing letters of application, doing community job surveys, engaging in dramatizations and role playing of job interviews and visiting numerous industries have aided in making this approach to information exploration useful.

3. *The Work Experience Seminar.*

Where students are involved in specialized work experience programs as part of the curriculum, the work experience seminar may be an effective device in furthering and developing information exploration and vocational decision-making.

4. *College Days.*

Faculty and guidance staff may organize special days on which representatives from post-high school institutions gather to present informative programs to students and meet with interested student groups for conferences.

5. *Career Days.*

Similar to college days, special time is set aside for personnel from business and industry, as well as other professions, to conduct workshops with students wishing to attend.

6. *Career Clubs.*

Students, faculty and guidance staff may participate in organizing career clubs to direct and immerse motivated participants in articulating and exploring individual educational and occupational goals.

7. *Student Forums.*

Student-faculty committees may be instituted to arrange special meeting times for the discussion of information-related topics. Properly structured with responsible student leaders, the student forum may interest members in furthering their use of available informational resources.

VII. TAXONOMY OF EDUCATIONAL AND VOCATIONAL WORLDS

The counselor must not only be aware of the informational materials available to him and his client, nor only of the particular counseling skills and techniques relevant to occupational and educational counseling, he must also develop some overall picture of the changing nature of the world of work and a broad picture of educational institutions and programs.

A. The Educational World

One of the most frequent ways of outlining the world of educational opportunities is given by Hollis and Hollis (1969, p. 80). It is an overview and serves only to provide a spectrum of educational institutions.

1. *Elementary and Secondary Schools.*
a. *Public.*

b. *Private.*
c. *Church-related.*
d. *Military.*
e. *Special.*
f. *Home study.*

2. *Occupationally Oriented Programs.*

   a. *On-the-job training.*
   b. *Apprenticeships.*
   c. *Vocational and trade schools.*
   d. *Business schools.*
   e. *Industrial training.*
   f. *Federal programs.*

3. *Higher Education.*

   a. *Junior and community colleges.*
   b. *Degree-granting colleges and universities.*

B. The World of Work

There are numerous ways of classifying the occupations in the United States, e.g. by functions performed, by interests, by abilities and aptitudes involved, etc. Two examples of classifications are given here, the first based upon the major industrial groups, the second, a more functional or psychological system, based upon levels of responsibility and skill involved in the occupation.

1. *Major Industrial Groups* (Bureau of Labor Statistics)

   a. *Agriculture, Forestry and Fisheries.*
   b. *Mining.*
   c. *Contract Construction.*
   d. *Manufacturing.*
   e. *Transportation and Public Utilities.*
   f. *Wholesale and Retail Trade.*
   g. *Finance, Insurance and Real Estate.*
   h. *Service and Miscellaneous.*
   i. *Government.*

2. *Levels of Responsibility and Skill* (Noris, Zeran & Hatch, 1966, pp. 106–107)

   a. *Professional and Managerial: Independent responsibility.*
   b. *Professional and Managerial; Narrower responsibilities than level a.*
   c. *Semi-professional and Small Business.*
   d. *Skilled.*
   e. *Semi-skilled.*
   f. *Unskilled.*

C. Trends and Change

The counselor acts as an observer of the changing worlds outside and attempts to take some responsibility for anticipating change and for predicting for his clients. He must know what trends are operating today which will change the lives of his clients tomorrow. Some trends which are apparent today are of interest (Hollis and Hollis, 1969).

1. *Education is increasingly becoming a continuing, on-going process of training and re-training rather than a terminal activity ending with a diploma.*
2. *Education is moving away from specific job-training to a kind of generalist activity in which flexibility to meet changing occupational needs is paramount.*
3. *Previously an individual held one occupation for most of his productive life. Increasingly the trends indicate he is likely to have three or more occupations in his own lifetime.*
4. *Long working periods are increasingly being shortened which results in either more leisure time or a greater probability that the individual will have two jobs simultaneously (moon-lighting).*

COMMENTARY: In sum, the guidance specialist must know the world of work and the major trends operating in it. He must be able to anticipate and predict for his clients. He must be able to provide a meaningful information service which gives the student an opportunity to explore occupational, educational and social information at his own level of readiness and maturity. He must function within guidance to help program information-exploration, either in the counseling relationship itself or by way of group guidance activities, career clubs, work experience seminars, etc. He must help maintain a valuable informational library which allows a student to experience broad, deep and personalized encounters with information corresponding to his specific educational, occupational or social interests and needs. He must attempt to keep this library supplied with up-dated and valid information which conforms to national standards of acceptability. He must frequently re-evaluate the kinds of information available and must develop an adequate system of information retrieval. This is fundamentally the nature and scope of the information service in guidance.

CHAPTER **10**

VOCATIONAL PLANNING, PLACEMENT AND FOLLOW-UP SERVICES

INTRODUCTION. If we consider informational inputs as a beginning kind of process of vocational exploration and planning, then placement and follow-up services are terminating points of this process. Each of these three services are activities within the sphere of the guidance function, although the counselor may not equally be involved in each. The degree of his participation in these service-activities depends upon whether there are other guidance personnel to design and administer such services. Whatever the role of the counselor and the degree of his participation, the guidance function is to maintain these three services activities at an effective level. Some treatment, therefore, is necessary on the rationale for maintaining vocational planning, placement and follow-up service as well as to briefly consider some fundamental features of the organization and administration of these guidance functions.

I. THE NEED FOR PLANNING, PLACEMENT AND FOLLOW-UP SERVICES

For vocational counseling to be effective, adequate attention should be given to short and long range career planning, student orientated placement and the follow-up study of the success and satisfaction of such placements. In our culture, education and economy are so rapidly changing that career decisions are made at earlier ages, even for occupations that have not yet been created. Keeping updated and abreast of changes and interpreting and communicating these changes to students is an over-all rationale for maintaining these services. However, there are specific factors to consider which make planning, placement and follow-up essential and necessary.

A. Changes in Occupational Outlooks

The future of different types of occupations is determined by and increasingly sensitive to a number of factors making effective planning and placement increasingly delicate.

1. *Fluctuations in the economy.*
2. *Changes in population.*
3. *Supply and demand of workers.*
4. *Supply and demand of goods and services.*
5. *Technological deevlopments and automation.*
6. *Seasonality of occupations.*
7. *The influence of international relations.*
8. *Legislation.*

B. General Increase of Knowledge

As man's population increases, so does the amount of knowledge that he possesses. Where an elementary school education was sufficient to enter the middle class many years ago, a college degree may be prerequisite in only a few years. Haphazard educational decisions in junior high school may now markedly affect future opportunities.

C. Socio-economic Disparities

Special groups of students require specialized planning and placement services. In order to eradicate some of our more outstanding social problems of poverty, delinquency and crime, special efforts must be made to help plan and implement vocational objectives for the underprivileged, the culturally disadvantaged, the handicapped, as well as the vocational aspirations of women.

D. The Military

The changing standards and requirements of the military services, the options provided special students for deferments, and the current changes in draft laws all point to the necessity of a well planned post high school decision.

II. PLACEMENT

The placement service attempts to assist students in post high school activities, and takes both an educational and occupational dimension. In terms of the former, the service provides for opportunities in junior colleges, colleges and universities as well as specialized technical training institutions. Occupational placement involves in-school and out-of-school, part-time and full-time placements.

A. Functions of the Placement Service

Though differences exist from school to school, some general functions of the placement service can be discerned.

1. *Involves itself in educational and occupational information exploration.*
2. *Conducts activities in job application, keeping a job, and providing opportunities for special groups.*
3. *Works closely with the State Employment Service.*
4. *Administers special programs e.g. work-experience programs, summer employment programs, etc.*
5. *Studies local and community resources and needs.*
6. *Observes laws and regulations concerning employment.*
    a. *Fair Labor Standards Act.*
    b. *Child labor laws.*
    c. *Hazardous-Occupations Orders.*
    d. *Employment certificates and work permits.*
    e. *State laws.*
    f. *Workmen's Compensation and Social Security.*
    g. *Income tax.*

B. Organization and Administration of Placement

The scope of the placement service depends on the resources of the school, the needs of the students and the community facilities which are available. The service can be organized according to a *centralized, decentralized* or *coordinated plan.* What is important in setting up the service is the proper selection of personnel and the delegation of responsibilities, the provision for adequate space for information, records, educational and employment forms, and job-order and referral forms.

III. FOLLOW-UP

Without some systematic knowledge of what students do and where they go after school, the placement service has little idea of its effectiveness or the areas in which it can improve. The follow-up program usually takes the form of a study, most frequently involving some staff constructed questionnaire. The contents of the follow-up survey depend on local considerations. However, some general guidelines have been offered to the planners of the follow-up survey.

A. **Purposes should be clear**

B. **Data obtained should satisfy stated purposes**

C. **The data-gathering instrument should be pilot tested before general administration**

D. **Sampling may be more efficient and economical than giving the instrument to everyone**

E. **Data should be amenable to statistical manipulation and analysis**

F. **Provisions should be made for those failing to respond**

CHAPTER **11**

RESEARCH AND EVALUATION IN COUNSELING AND GUIDANCE

INTRODUCTION. Many professionals in the guidance movement reflect a profound need for more research and evaluation of guidance programs and services. Evaluation is a term which refers to a systematic assessment of the effectiveness with which goals are achieved. Since schools have varying goals in the provision of their guidance services, the programs for systematic evaluation of these goals tend to be equally varied. Only through well thought out evaluation programs can a basis be laid for the improvement of services to students.

I. EVALUATION APPROACHES

In deciding what approach to use in evaluation, certain basic considerations should be given attention. The problems and goals must be clearly defined, and the evaluative criteria listed. More importantly, the planning of the evaluation should be done by qualified staff.

A. Case Study

As reviewed in the chapter on nontest techniques of appraisal, the case study is an individualized means of gauging the effect of some variable on student progress. While the case study method is well suited to evaluating the counseling process and the techniques of the counselor, it is too time consuming to evaluate other aspects of the guidance program.

B. Survey

A survey is the most economical and popular method of gathering evaluative information. The survey defines a list of criteria which it wishes to examine and is so constructed as to collect enough data upon which judgments can be made about the effectiveness of programs, the needs of the school or how worthwhile certain activities are for the students.

C. Experimental Method

An experimental procedure is more sophisticated as a method in evaluation. It is a highly rigorous means of assessing limited and well defined variables. Its advantage lies in economy in that samples of students may be used to provide information rather than the whole student population. Its disadvantage is found, however, in its restrictiveness, its complexity and in the fact that qualified guidance personnel are not always available for its proper administration.

II. EVALUATIVE CRITERIA

The key to successful and meaningful evaluation depends largely on the criteria which are used in the study. These criteria may be internal or external, general or specific, relevant or irrelevant. Only by proper planning can criteria be selected which will have meaning for the school over time.

A. General Criteria

1. *Reduced student failure.*
2. *Fewer disciplinary actions.*
3. *Increased use of guidance services.*
4. *Degree to which programs serve student needs.*
5. *Flexibility of staff and services.*
6. *Cooperation and effective communication among staff.*
7. *Accessibility and availability of materials and resources.*
8. *Availability of guidance services at all levels.*
9. *Maintenance and utilization of personal appraisal data.*

B. Specific Criteria

Some evaluative criteria are more related to certain guidance services than others.

1. *Counseling: External Criteria*

   a. *Counselor-student ratio* (suggested 1: 250 to 300).
   b. *Qualified and certified counselors.*
   c. *Communication of counselor role.*
   d. *Percentage of noncounseling duties engaged in.*
   e. *Proportion of student self-referrals.*

2. *Educational-vocational Services.*

   a. *Student grade point averages.*
   b. *Job satisfaction.*
   c. *Amount of earnings.*
   d. *Persistence in post-high school activities.*
   e. *Number of drop-outs.*

3. *Information Services.*

   a. *Proportion of students using materials.*
   b. *Effectiveness of informational guidance activities.*
   c. *Effectiveness of orientation programs.*

4. *Placement and Follow-up Services.*

   a. *Coordination of placement services with local and state employment services.*
   b. *Number of follow-up studies conducted.*
   c. *Percentage of graduates employed in chosen field.*

5. *Other Services.*

The evaluative criteria of other school services, e.g. administration or instruction may also be part of the evaluation study. It should be noted, however, that the criteria listed here are just some of many which have been used. By no means do they constitute the total supply of criteria available for evaluation studies. The best criteria are those which are meaningful for the school in its own unique milieu.

III. EVALUATION OF THE COUNSELING PROCESS

If counseling is a science, its procedures must ultimately be based upon testable and verifiable assumptions. Does counseling work? If so, does it work with all clients? If not, which clients and which type of counselor or counseling approach is most effective? These questions can only be answered using an *experimental* method in a systematic evaluation of counseling. This type of research is also called *outcome* research. Review of systematic studies of counseling outcomes depends upon outside reading. General problems and characteristics of outcome research in counseling may be treated here, however.

A. Problems in Selecting Variables

The goal or outcome of counseling depends upon the theoretical orientation of the counselor, the wishes of the client and the setting in which they interact. The list of possible counseling outcomes is inexhaustible. Some outcomes are listed.

1. *Reduction in anxiety.*
2. *Greater spontaneity.*
3. *Greater self-acceptance.*
4. *Improved ego strength.*
5. *Greater tolerance for ambiguity.*
6. *Improved self-control.*
7. *Reduced defensiveness.*
8. *Improved interpersonal relationships.*
9. *Specific behavioral change.*
10. *Reduction of irrational behavior.*

B. Problems in Measuring Selected Variables

In order to evaluate counseling, the usual design is to measure some variable, e.g. anxiety, before and after counseling and to make a comparison of these pre- and post-tests to measure differences which may be attributable to the counseling relationship which has intervened between them. Not all the variables one has selected, however, are measurable, nor are they all *unambiguous, reliable* and *observable*. Selecting appropriate comparison variables, therefore, depends upon meeting a number of criteria before they can be used in an experimental investigation.

C. Problems in Controlling Extraneous Variables

A client in counseling may experience the death of a parent or a serious illness. This intervening event may radically effect the content and outcome of the counseling relationship. In an experimental study, where a group of clients is observed over a definite period of time, certain extraneous factors must be controlled to properly evaluate the impact of the counselor and the relationship upon the client. Often this is done by matching clients with other clients not receiving treatment or by using various *control groups*. It is assumed that these "extraneous" variables are equally likely to effect the control group as the experimental group. Differences obtained between the groups, therefore, are more likely to be due to the experimental treatment, (counseling) and not due to these outside factors. Control groups, however, are difficult to obtain, organize, measure, and follow over time for counselor's working in a field situation.

D. Problems in Scoring, Analyzing and Interpreting Obtained Data

Often scoring a measure of change in counseling, e.g. "spontoneity" depends upon observer judgment and is frequently a matter of subjectivity and experimental bias. Assuming data is scored and collected adequately, however, additional problems occur in selecting appropriate statistical tests to measure important differences. Certain statistical tests are impractical without the aid of computing services. Once the data has been obtained, scored and computed, moreover, the task of interpreting what the data indicates, if it is valid data, whether the data answers the question posed originally by the study, is a crucial last step in producing a meaningful evaluation of counseling outcomes.

PART III

THE COUNSELING FUNCTION

CHAPTER **12**

THE SCHOOL COUNSELOR

INTRODUCTION. The effect of federal support for guidance activities, as well as the myriad social forces facilitating the growth of guidance, has led to the professional development of school counseling both in quality and in number. This momentum, however, has left in its wake a complex pattern of changing needs, requirements, professional standards and responsibilities.

I. THE NEED FOR COUNSELORS

Needs are difficult to assess as they depend upon role definitions, methods of tabulation and the selection of criteria upon which projections of needs in future years are made.

A. Counselor-student Ratio

In the late fifties the ratio of counselor to pupils was somewhere near 1 to 900. In 1964 the ratio had declined to 1 to 500 in the secondary school. It should be noted, however, that these figures do not imply an even distribution throughout the fifty states. The recommended counselor-student ratio is approximately 1 to 300 for secondary schools, from 1 to 300 to 1 to 600 at elementary levels and 1 to 750 for colleges.

B. Supply and Demand

Using the above ratios, it has been estimated that a shortage of 60,000 to 80,000 counselors existed in 1970, and that the increase in certified counselors was just keeping pace with the growth in population.

II. PREPARATION OF COUNSELORS

The difficulties in evaluating counselor effectiveness has led to

113

a feeling that more attention be given to what characteristics a counselor should have and what are the best ways to train him (Schertzer & Stone, 1968).

A.　Selection

Typically counselors have emerged from the ranks of teachers. This tendency has not been viewed as necessarily desirable when it is not accompanied by other characteristics. The *American College Personnel Association* has recommended certain guidelines for the selection of candidates for graduate training in counseling. Some of these are abstracted below.

1. *Above average intelligence and achievement.*
2. *A scientific attitude.*
3. *Knowledge of cognate fields.*
4. *Demonstrated and appraised counseling interests.*
5. *Emotional stability and adjustment.*
6. *One year of teaching or related experience.*

B.　Program Content

Although states differ in certification requirements and universities in program requirements, it is generally assumed that a counselor should possess a Master's degree, and that his academic preparation include a distribution of work in at least three basic areas.

1. *Psychology.*
    a. *Child and adolescent development.*
    b. *Individual differences.*
    c. *Learning.*
    d. *Personality.*

2. *Education.*
    a. *Philosophy and history.*
    b. *Curriculum and administration.*
    c. *Educational measurement.*

3. *Counseling and Guidance.*
    a. *Foundations and principles.*

b. *Appraisal.*
c. *Counseling.*
d. *Vocational development.*
e. *Group procedures.*
f. *Supervised counseling practicum.*

C. Quality of Preparation

In general certain patterns have emerged to define a high character in counselor preparation. These basic elements must still be viewed as an ideal rather than a reality, although the profession is rapidly moving to achieve it.

1. *A minimum two-year degree program which is sequential.*
2. *A behavioral science core.*
3. *Supervised practicum and internship experiences.*
4. *Opportunities for personal development.*

III. CERTIFICATION OF SCHOOL COUNSELORS

Certification requirements vary from state to state. At the beginning of 1960 only thirty-five states had mandatory certification requirements.

A. Reasons for Certification

Generally a state makes certification requirements to assure some degree of quality control. In some states certification requirements are influenced by other considerations.

1. *Raise standards.*
2. *Provide selection guidelines.*
3. *Facilitate professional status of counseling.*
4. *Influence counselor training.*
5. *Establish uniformity in preparation and practice.*

B. Basic Requirements

Despite the wide variance in requirements from state to state, the typical certification plan includes most of the following criteria.

1. *Teaching experience.*

2. *A teaching certificate.*
3. *Hour requirements in guidance course work.*

IV. COUNSELOR FUNCTION AND ROLE

Just what do counselors do? This question represents a focus of conflict within and outside the profession. Pupils, teachers, administrators, parents, superintendents and federal funding agencies have varying perceptions of what counselors ought to do. Some of these points of conflict will be reviewed in the chapter on *Issues in Guidance.* For the present, a review of the school counselor's own statement of his role, as given by the *American School Counselors Association* (ASCA) will serve to illustrate the scope of his functions in the school.

A. Planning the Guidance Program

The counselor plays a central role in planning and developing the services and procedures to be used in the overall guidance program.

B. Counseling

The majority of the school counselor's time should be devoted to individual and small-group counseling activities.

C. Appraisal

The counselor plays a major role in the accumulation, organization and interpretation of appraisal data gathered from students.

D. Vocational Planning

The counselor must assume responsibility for some part in the provision of educational and occupational information and counseling services.

E. Referrals

The counselor acts in the pupil personnel team as one co-ordinator of referrals both within the school and with outside agencies.

F. Placements

Another responsibility assumed by the counselor is the provision of adequate educational and occupational placement services for all students requiring assistance.

G. Parent Assistance

The counselor stands as a resource person to assist parents and interpret guidance activities to them.

H. Consultant

The counselor provides a consulting function to teachers, administrators and other guidance staff on individual pupils.

I. Research

The counselor helps to determine local research needs and assists in the implementation of these studies.

V. LEGAL AND ETHICAL BASES FOR COUNSELING

A counselor exists in a social context. Frequently the school counselor finds himself in a complex network of responsibilities, role conflicts and administrative, professional and legal limitations on his functioning. An awareness of these restrictions is imperative for any form of professional practice (Schmidt, 1962).

A. Privileged Communication and Confidentiality

Privileged communication is a more specific legal term than confidentiality. The legal aspect of a confidential relationship implies that there is no disclosure of information to individuals not entitled to it either verbally or in written form. A privileged communication is a confidential communication which need not be revealed at a judicial proceeding. Differences in state laws make it difficult to determine to what degree the state provides for confidentiality and privileged communication for the counselor and his client.

B. Expert Witness

An expert witness is a person designated to be qualified to

give testimony which requires some special knowledge, skill or training. Psychiatrists and psychologists are often called to testify in cases of criminal responsibility as expert witnesses. Vocational counselors have been used as expert witnesses in cases involving the processing of claims for disability insurance.

C. Slander and Libel

A person can be awarded damages by a court to the degree that he has experienced mental suffering or loss of reputation as a result of defamation in the revealing of information to a third party. Libel is written defamation, slander spoken. The implications for the counselor are that counseling records must be prepared with caution with deliberate considerations being given to what is said about an individual in the relationship, and the degree to which these remarks could be interpreted as damaging, defamatory and untrue.

D. Right of Privacy

The right of privacy is the constitutional guarantee against invasion or intrusion into one's private affairs. The essence of the right is the basic freedom of the person to choose the times and circumstances where his attitudes, behavior or feelings are to be shared or withheld from others. In administering research devices or appraisal instruments in which such personal matters are tapped, the counselor must conscientiously observe each person's right against invasion of privacy.

E. Malpractice

Any misconduct or unreasonable lack of competency in carrying out professional duties is referred to as malpractice. A failure to recognize the limitations placed upon the counselor in terms of the specifications of his competencies and professional roles may lead to his operating in spheres not protected by any legal precedents. In such cases the counselor may be subject to civil and criminal liabilities.

F. Ethical Standards

Most ethical issues center around a conflict in responsibilities for the counselor. On the one hand he exists in an institutional setting and has responsibilities to that institution and to society as a whole. On the other hand, his client may place him in a position in which the institution may be hurt or damaged, but the obvious reciprocal damage wrought on the client by the disclosure of some information to the institution might be equally great. Such problems of responsibilities, confidentiality and other ethical matters are treated in the publication by the *American Personnel and Guidance Association* "Ethical Standards." Every practicing counselor should have examined this document with care for his own protection.

CHAPTER **13**

COUNSELING I:
SYSTEMS AND THEORIES

INTRODUCTION. A theory or system of counseling is a means of organizing facts, principles and procedures into a meaningful, internally consistent approach toward a client. It may incorporate a theory of personality or a philosophical view of man. The purpose of this chapter is to review the most relevant counseling theories, to delineate what counseling is and how it is conceptualized within each system, and to look at how each of the counseling approaches is implemented with a client or class of clients. Before considering these systems, however, it is necessary to examine a basic definition of counseling and how counseling is differentiated from psychotherapy.

I. DEFINITION OF COUNSELING

One of the most central aspects of any definition of counseling is that it involves some type of *helping relationship between a counselor and client*. From this starting point counseling definitions share less and less in common. Most tend to depend upon the particular theory in which they are imbedded. Some general features of these definitions, however, usually incorporate the following concepts.

A. Facilitating Behavior Change
In many different ways the counselor's function is to provide conditions which facilitate a change in client behavior.

B. Establishing Limits
The values and approach of the counselor, as well as the choices of the client, serve to define the goals of the relationship and impose limitations on it.

C. Understanding and Listening

Regardless of the theoretical bias of the counselor, most counseling theories stress the importance of understanding and listening in the relationship.

D. Privacy and Confidentiality

The counseling relationship is always conducted in an atmosphere of mutual respect and discretion. Without privacy and confidentiality, trust and openness are severely inhibited.

II. COUNSELING VERSUS PSYCHOTHERAPY

One point of controversy between these two disciplines is whether there is a difference between them and, if so, in what respects. Some suggested points of divergence are worth observing.

A. Clients and Problems

Typically it is said that counseling deals with normal clients having adjustment and problem-solving difficulties, while psychotherapy deals with individuals having some deficiencies or handicaps. This position leads to the view that counseling is a form of psychotherapy but confined to normal clients.

B. Qualities of the Relationship

Counseling is often viewed in terms of maintaining supportive, palliative, educative, counselor-client relationships while psychotherapy is more remedial and reconstructive, focusing on depth factors in the relationship and participating to a greater degree in the emotional dimension of the interaction.

C. Training

The counselor is most often trained at the master's level while the psychotherapist may have doctoral level training and some amount of supervised post-doctoral internship experience.

D. Setting

The psychotherapeutic setting is often in the clinic or hospital environment while the counselor most often functions in educational settings.

III.　CLASSIFICATION OF COUNSELING APPROACHES

The variety of counseling systems and theories has itself resulted in a variety of classification schemes. Two such groupings are reviewed.

A.　Philosophical grouping (Blocher, 1966)

Some writers have attempted to group counseling theories into their major philosophical families. Three major categories have been derived.

1. *Essentialism.*

The main elements of essentialism are the emphasis upon reason and the objectivity of reality. In this system values may be universal and absolutes understandable. The counseling approach which derives from this orientation is a directive one in which certain "known" bits of information are communicated to the client about his personality, attitudes, etc. *Rational* and *trait-factor* counseling models usually fit into this essentialist orientation.

2. *Progressivism.*

In contrast to essentialism, progressivism sees reality more subjectively, with truth and values contingent upon experiences of the individual. *Pragmatism* and *experimentalism* would exemplify this philosophical style. Learning theory and some social-interpersonal counseling approaches would probably be fit into this approach.

3. *Existentialism.*

Most subjective in its view of reality, existentialism is based upon an individual's tenuousness and freedom. Humanism is frequently an accompanying feature of this approach. A wide definition of existentialism may be able to include phenomenological counseling approaches as well as existential ones.

B. Theoretical Groupings

The most frequent classificatory scheme for counseling theories is to group them in terms of their overall theoretical orientation. The major designations here are *trait-factor* or *rational* approaches, *learning or neo-behavioral* approaches *psychoanalytic, perceptual-phenomenological* and *existential* approaches.

COUNSELING THEORIES

I. TRAIT-FACTOR OR RATIONAL APPROACH TO COUNSELING

The trait-factor approach is the most directive and didactic model. It assumes that, through certain objective means, those underlying traits and characteristics of an individual may be observed and communicated to the counselee to aid him in adjusting to and planning in his environment.

A. Edmund G. Williamson

Williamson finds his historical roots in the Parsonian approach. Formerly his model focused upon vocational development. It has now been broadened to include a more comprehensive picture of the individual in counseling. Williamson conceives of counseling as a task of assessing the individual's assets and liabilities with objective measures to aid him in making appropriate vocational and life decisions. The objective of counseling is the achievement of self-controlled, forward development of client potentialities. The counselor is seen somewhat as an expert who appraises the client's traits, develops a profile of the client and helps him to see himself in his environment appropriately and accurately so he can make meaningful decisions about his future. Fundamentally, the counseling relationship is a remedial one between a *mentor and a learner.* The counselor brings scientific and objective techniques to bear upon the client and *directs* him through the process of decision-making and adjustment.

1. *Counseling Process.*

Williamson conceives of trait-factor counseling as a six stage affair.

a. *Analysis*. The counselor collects data from interviews and psychological tests and uses a case study approach towards a beginning understanding of the client.

b. *Synthesis*. The data gathered on the client is organized and summarized in such a way that strengths and weaknesses are apparent.

c. *Diagnosis*. The counselor formulates tentative conclusions about the client, his problems, their underlying significance and dynamics.

d. *Prognosis*. On the basis of the diagnostic conclusions the counselor predicts the client's future development and draws out implications from the diagnosis which bear upon the client's future directions.

e. *Counseling*. This limited definition of counseling refers to the process of facilitating the client's adjustment or readjustment, to marshal his own resources and those of his environment to achieve optimum development.

f. *Follow-up*. This process evaluates effectiveness of decisions made in the counseling process and assists the client when new problems arise.

2. *Techniques of counseling.*

Many techniques are used with clients in this system and a certain flexibility must characterize their use inasmuch as they depend upon the individual client. However, the techniques which are used tend to fall into five general areas of implementation (Patterson, 1966).

a. *Establishing rapport.*
b. *Cultivating self-understanding.*
c. *Advising or planning a program of action.*
d. *Carrying out the plan.*
e. *Referral, where appropriate.*

B.   Frederick C. Thorne

Founder of the *Journal of Clinical Psychology*, Frederick Thorne identifies himself as an *eclectic* counselor, i.e. one who uses techniques and methods from various systems, the choice dependent upon the nature of the disorder, the type of action needed, etc. His system of *personality counseling* is often termed a rational approach in that he sees the counseling process as a process of *re-education and learning* with emphasis placed upon the individual's maximal use of his *intellectual resources* to achieve adjustment and effective problem-solving behavior. Thorne sees eclectic counseling as based upon a principle of flexibility and that counseling techniques will be selected only after a scientific process of data collection and diagnosis has resulted in a positive identification of the client's disorder. Techniques used may be classified on an active-passive continuum (Thorne, 1961).

1. *Active techniques.*
   a. Suggestion.
   b. Persuasion.
   c. Pressure.
   d. Coercion.

2. *Passive, non-directive techniques.*
   a. Listening.
   b. Acceptance.
   c. Reflection.
   d. Clarification.
   e. Catharsis.

C. Albert Ellis

The *rational emotive therapy* (RET) of Albert Ellis takes the position that all *neurotic behavior results from illogical thinking.* The task of therapy is to identify and eliminate these irrational attitudes, substituting rational ideas for them. The therapist acts as a counter propagandist who contradicts each irrational or superstitious thought pattern in the client with unrelenting persuasion. Further, he often insists that the client engage in activity which he fears in order to eradicate the irrational behavioral process as well.

1. *The ABC theory.*

The A-B-C theory of personality and behavior shows how the

development of neurotic behavior proceeds. 'A' is the existence of a fact, behavior or attitude of another person. 'C' is the reaction of the individual which follows from the behavior of the person in question, e.g. a reaction such as grief or unhappiness. While it appears that A causes C, i.e. that a person behaves in such a way as to cause unhappiness in another person, that in fact there is an intervening condition, 'B'. 'B' is the individual's *self-verbalization* or *interpretation* of 'A' which results in the unhappiness or emotional disturbance, 'C'. These irrational self-verbalizations are called superstitions. Ellis lists eleven.

2. *Eleven irrational superstitions* (B).

a. It is essential that one be loved or approved by virtually everyone in his community.

b. One must be perfectly competent, adequate and achieving to consider oneself worthwhile.

c. Some people are bad, wicked or villainous and therefore should be blamed and punished.

d. It is a terrible catastrophe when things are not as one wants them to be.

e. Unhappiness is caused by outside circumstances, and the individual has no control over it.

f. Dangerous or fearsome things are causes for great concern and their possibility must be continually dwelt upon.

g. It is easier to avoid certain difficulties and self responsibilities than to face them.

h. One should be dependent on others and must have someone stronger on whom to rely.

i. Past experiences and events are the determiners of present behavior; the influence of the past cannot be eradicated.

j. One should be quite upset over other people's problems and disturbances.

k. There is always a right or perfect solution to every problem, and it must be found or the results will be catastrophic. (Patterson, 1966, pp. 110–112)

3. *Nature of neurosis.*

Continuing or chronic states of emotional upheaval or disturbance are determined, therefore, not by external situations or events (A), but by the individual's perceptions, attitudes and interpretations of these events which are internalized, self-defeating, superstitious and irrational self-verbalizations. The task of therapy is to attack and replace these superstitious systems with rational ones.

II. LEARNING THEORY OR NEO-BEHAVIORAL APPROACH TO COUNSELING

While there are many types of learning approaches to counseling and psychotherapy, there are fundamental similarities in orientation. All change in behavior is a result of either growth, lesions or learning. Most behavior is learned in the form of habits which may be either adaptive or maladaptive. Neurotic behavior is seen as a system of maladaptive habits which must be unlearned. A further common element to this approach is that the learned behavior dealt with in the counseling setting must be observable behavior just as the techniques employed to alter these behaviors must be scientifically replicable. Learning and behavioral approaches stress a rigid experimental attitude. Counseling is an applied science.

A. Andrew Salter

Salter uses a *conditioned reflex approach* in counseling which derives from some of Pavlov's ideas. His view of neurosis is that it results from environmental conditioning in which *inhibition* plays too dominant a role. Therapy consists of changing inhibitory individuals into excitatory, spontaneous persons. The techniques employed revolve around increasing excitation. Such techniques as *feeling-talk,* uttering spontaneous feelings, *facial-talk,* showing emotions in facial expressions, *improvisation, contradiction* and *attack* are means of achieving a greater excitatory potential in the inhibited client (Salter, 1949). The approach is frequently criticized for its over-simplification of complex behavior problems.

B. Joseph Wolpe

Neurotic behavior is learned behavior conforming to causal

laws. Since anxiety frequently accompanies neurosis, the behaviors which elicit the anxiety may be treated using the technique of *reciprocal inhibition*. Reciprocal inhibition is the weakening of old responses by new ones. Wolpe, however, has helped develop a more general *behavior therapy*, and some of its more basic concepts are worth noting.

1. *Basic concepts of behavior therapy* (Wolpe, and Lazarus, 1966).

a. *Counterconditioning*. If a response which is inhibitory to, or counter to, an anxiety response can be made to occur in the presence of anxiety evoking stimuli, then the previous bond between those stimuli and the anxiety response they elicit will be reduced and weakened. This is the principle of counterconditioning and reciprocal inhibition.

b. *Positive reconditioning*. This term refers to the conditioning of new motor habits or ways of thinking in order to overcome particular maladaptive reaction patterns.

c. *Experimental extinction*. A habit is weakened or extinguished by repeated non-reinforcement. A child who teases other children in a classroom in order to get the teacher's attention, for example, may decrease the frequency of this behavior when that reinforcement is withdrawn, and the teacher ignores the child's teasing.

2. *Techniques of behavior therapy.*

After a lengthy procedure of data gathering and appraisal, accompanied by history-taking interviews, appropriate treatment plans are made and techniques selected. Some behavior therapy techniques are abstracted below (Wolpe and Lazarus, 1966).

a. *Assertive training*. Inhibitory individuals are encouraged to engage in assertive behaviors. Each time the patient expresses feelings which were formerly inhibited, his expression reciprocally inhibits the anxiety which prevented them from coming out. Assertive responses grow in strength as they increase in frequency. Specific assertive techniques include the *reconditioning techniques* of Salter, the use of *behavioral rehearsal* or *role playing* and the generalization of these responses into the patient's life situation. Assertive responses are best utilized gradually with easy tasks preceding more difficult ones.

b. *Sexual responses.* Sexual arousal is in itself antagnostic to anxiety; however, anxiety responses are often conditioned to sexual stimuli. With problems of sexual inadequacy, e.g. impotence, premature ejaculation, retarded ejaculation, etc., the patient is told to engage in sexual activity only as far as it is predominantly pleasurable. His partner must collaborate to give him this flexibility. He gradually increases his sexual activity as his anxiety is inhibited.

c. *Respiratory responses.* Individuals in a state of panic or pervasive anxiety, where anxiety evoking stimuli are not known, may be taught to breathe deeply as this often reduces the anxiety state. A mixture of *carbon dioxide and oxygen* (65% to 35%) may also be used, and this procedure has been effective in reducing free-floating anxiety states.

d. *Abreaction.* In cases where anxiety-evoking stimuli are not known, the therapist may wish to have the patient return to and re-evoke the fearful past experience. Many techniques are used to plunge the patient into this kind of cathartic state: *hypnosis,* the use of *di-ethyl ether, LSD, methedrine,* etc.

e. *Systematic Desensitization.* This procedure is the most highly developed behavior therapy technique. The basic aim of the process is the reduction of anxiety and the weakening of anxiety evoking stimuli. Three basic procedures are involved.

(1) *Training in relaxation.* The patient is trained, usually in about six sessions, to learn a state of deep muscular relaxation.

(2) *Construction of anxiety hierarchies.* The therapist attempts, through a series of interviews and questionnaires, to develop a *graded list of stimuli* which evoke anxiety in the patient.

(3) *Counterposing relaxation and anxiety evoking stimuli.* The individual in a state of deep relaxation, is asked to imagine the weakest item on the anxiety hierarchy. If he can do so without anxiety arousal, he proceeds to imagine the next strongest item. Counterposing increasingly

stronger anxiety evoking stimuli with relaxation responses apparently results in desensitization or weakening of the bond between these stimulus situations and the anxiety response.

III. PSYCHOANALYTIC APPROACHES TO COUNSELING

The origin of the psychoanalytic movement is traced to Freud. The major elements of the theory involve the propositions that all behavior is caused, that a great share of behavior is motivated by unconscious forces, and that sexuality plays a large part in shaping neurotic problems. The applications of psychoanalysis to counseling have been often limited since fewer sessions and less depth differentiate a counseling relationship from an analytic one. Some adaptation of psychoanalytic principles to the world of counseling, however, has occurred; two such systems are reviewed.

A. Edward S. Bordin (Bordin, 1955)

Bordin sees counseling as more than simply re-educative or remedial activity but one which involves emotional and motivational elements. It is to be differentiated from psychotherapy, however, in that it tends to be *less ambiguous, more cognitive* and somewhat *less emotional* than psychotherapy. Bordin's model is called *psychological counseling*, and it is psychoanalytic insofar as it sees personality in a *central* rather than peripheral way in the counseling process. The individual's personality is organized as a system of impulses, attitudes, and emotions following many of the conceptualizations in psychoanalysis (id, ego, superego, etc.). *Diagnosis*, therefore, plays an important role in the process of psychological counseling inasmuch as it facilitates awareness on the part of the counselor of the underlying nuclear impulses and needs in the client.

1. *Dimensions of counseling.*

The counseling process may be viewed in terms of three major dimensions.

a. *Ambiguity*. Ambiguity is a lack of structure or direction in therapy. The greater the lack of structure, the more likely the client will project his own irrational feelings and attitudes into the therapeutic milieu, revealing unconscious material important for therapeutic analysis. Counseling is less ambiguous than psychotherapy, more structured and consequently does not delve as deeply into projected unconscious material as psychotherapy does.

b. *Cognitive-conative balance.* Counseling is distinguished as maintaining a balance between intellectual, or cognitive processes, and affective, or conative ones. Therapy is not entirely intellectualized and insight-oriented; neither is it purely a cathartic emotional release. Instead, it seeks to give the individual a structured and organized emotional experience which is therapeutic, a balance between intellectual and affective processes.

c. *Emotional tone.* The relationship between counselor and client is characterized by certain facilitative emotional dynamics. The counselor must keep a certain detachment or *objectivity*, but at the same time, he cannot be aloof and indifferent for to some extent, he must experience an *involvment* in the client's emotional struggle. Further, the counselor must evidence *warmth* towards his client; this may merely be the counselor's willingness to be free and spontaneous in his own reactivity with the client.

A final emotional dynamic in the relationship is *support* and *reassurrance*. While some clients may feel stifled by such an element in the relationship, others may need such palliative treatment. The amount of support and reassurance provided by the counselor is based on the needs of the client.

2. *Counseling techniques.*

The number of therapeutic procedures is kept to a minimum in psychological counseling; further, they tend to be dictated by the client and to some degree are dependent upon the reason the client entered the relationship (vocational counseling, personal counseling, etc.).

a. *Testing and diagnosis.* Vocational counseling particularly necessitates the use of testing, the appropriate selections of tests and the therapeutic interpretation of test results. Even in nonvocational counseling, however, the counselor may use appraisal devices to diagnose the client's needs, but these devices tend to be more counselor-centered and may not involve direct test interpretation with the client.

b. *Acceptance and Understanding.* The objective of counseling is to have the client reveal himself to the counselor. By providing a warm and accepting environment and by communicating understanding, the counselor helps develop rapport with the client, and this forms the basis of the relationship.

c. *Interpretation.* The most viable therapeutic tool is interpretation. It usually occurs later in the relationship when the client is relatively free with the counselor and trusting enough to express important feelings. Through appropriate timing of new insights and clarifications of important explicit and implicit feelings the client has expressed, the counselor facilitates the client's development of a new awareness of himself, his reaction patterns, his defensive adjustments and his relationship patterns with the counselor.

B. Franz Alexander

Alexander's *psychoanalytic therapy* is relevant to counseling in that it stresses a brief encounter between therapist and client, an abbreviated form of psychoanalysis. Fundamental adherence to Freud's concepts of *psychosexual development,* the mental structures of *id, ego* and *superego* and the *defense mechanism of the ego* are all found in Alexander's approach. Psychoanalytic theory differs from psychoanalysis, however, in at least three ways: (a) it stresses a briefer encounter between therapist and patient, (b) its therapeutic plan is flexible and varies from client to client rather than posing as a standard form of treatment for all clients, and (c) it attempts to provide a *corrective emotional experience* for the individual rather than emphasizing the importance of intellectual insight into one's psychodynamics as orthodox analysis might. Apart from these modifications in psychoanalytic technique, it is highly psychoanalytically oriented at a theoretical and diagnostic level (Alexander, 1946).

1. *Nature of therapy.*

The goal of therapy is to restore the person's mental health as this relates to both internal and external worlds. Typically it involves the bringing of unconscious material into the conscious awareness of the client. Three elements in this effort are worth observing.

a. *Emotional abreaction.* Part of therapy consists of having the individual emotionally re-experience the hidden and perhaps traumatic emotional experiences which his ego has heretofore denied from awareness or expression. Catharsis is an essential element of this model.

b. *Intellectual insight.* As new denied and repressed material is expressed, the individual expands his awareness and develops deeper insight into his personality structure and neurosis.

c. *Recollection of the repressed.* Since psychoanalysis conceives of neurotic problems as having their basis in repression, the ultimate objective of therapy is to recover these hidden feelings and experience and bring them into the intellectual and emotional spheres of awareness, freeing or liberating the patient from the self-defeating nature of repression.

2. Techniques of therapy.

The therapist begins treatment by first using tests, interviews and other appraisal devices to make a preliminary diagnosis of the patient's problem and intrapsychic structure. He develops a *plan of treatment,* individually suited to the patient, and works toward the achievement of limited therapeutic objectives. While therapy depends upon individual clients, some general psychoanalytic techniques may be employed.

a. *Free association.* The fundamental rule of psychoanalysis, free association is a technique in which the patient is asked to allow any thought or impulse into consciousness and to feel free to express any ideas regardless of their consequences. This method facilitates the client's revelation of unconscious material, repressed memories, forbidden fantasies, etc.

b. *Transference.* The client often transfers many of his irrational feelings and attitudes onto the therapist; these are relatively stereotyped reaction patterns and are thus inappropriate to the relationship. Differentiating the therapist from the transference neurosis is a major element of therapy.

c. *Interpretation.* Often unconscious material which comes out of free association or the transference, is not understood by the patient. The analyst uses interpretation frequently to offer insight to the patient, to help him develop new cognitions and to see his impulses in new ways. Interpretations are a major tool of psychoanalytic therapy; they point out connections between conscious and unconscious elements and thereby help liberate the patient from the dominance of unconscious complexes.

d. *Dream Interpretation.* Like free association, a dream reveals unconscious or latent impulses and wishes. Further, it reveals how the individual deals with his forbidden impulse network, i.e. whether he represses, projects, denies, etc. The analyst works with the patient to uncover the latent meaning of dreams, to understand their implications in conscious life and to interpret their significance into the life situation of the individual.

e. *Other techniques.* The therapist may manipulate the *frequency of sessions* with the client to control the amount of dependency the therapy may encourage; *interruptions* in therapy may be called for to eventually prepare the way for termination of treatment. Furthermore, manipulating interview-frequency and interrupting treatment may effect the tranference relationship in ways which may be meaningfully interpreted to the client. These techniques tend not to be characteristic of orthodox psychoanalysis and are means by which the psychoanalytic therapy of Alexander may be more abbreviated, efficient and economical than the traditional analytic relationship which is usually longer, deeper and more heavily involved in transference interpretation (Patterson, 1966).

IV. PERCEPTUAL-PHENOMENOLOGICAL APPROACHES TO COUNSELING

Whereas the behavioral approach emphasizes observable, external behaviors, the *perceptual-phenomenological* approach (also called self-theory) stresses the subjective, internal perceptual organization of the individual. Each person sees his world differently in his own unique phenomenal field of experience, and it is this frame of reference which governs an individual's actions in the world. The most extensive development of this model is given by Carl Rogers, although other phenomenological theorists are worth investigation.

A. Carl Rogers

The client-centered counseling approach developed by Rogers is frequently used in school counseling. The basic attitude toward the individual is that each man must be respected for his own *uniqueness*, his *capacity for self direction* and his fundamental *worth and significance*. The client centered therapist does not advise or interpret in order to help the client, but makes the assumption that the individual has a fundamental synthetic tendency to *unify and integrate his self structure* and to *actualize his potentialities*.

1. *Necessary conditions for therapy to occur.*

For therapy and personality change to occur, only six conditions must be fulfilled in the client- counselor relationship. These conditions are both necessary and sufficient.

a. Two persons are in contact;

b. One, the client, is in a state of incongruence, being vulnerable or anxious;

c. the other, therapist, is congruent in the relationship;

d. the therapist experiences unconditional positive regard toward the client.

e. The therapist experiences an empathic understanding of the client's internal frame of reference;

f. the client perceives, at least to a minimal degree, conditions (4) and (5) (Rogers, 1959 p. 216). (Conditions 4 and 5 refer to items d and e in the outline.)

2. *Process theory of psychotherapy.*

Rogers sees the therapy process occurring in a series of stages which are experienced by the client. Patterson (1966) summarizes these stages of the therapy process.

a. A loosening of feelings.

b. A change in the manner of experiencing.

c. A shift from incongruence to congruence.

d. A change in the manner in which and the extent to which the individual is willing and able to communicate himself in a receptive climate.

e. A loosening of the cognitive maps of experience.

f. A change in the individual's relationship to his problem.

g. A change in the individual's manner of relating. (p. 419)

3. *Techniques of client-centered counseling.*

The client enters the counseling relationship with some incongruence between himself and his experience from which threat and vulnerability result. The objective of therapy is to facilitate his becoming more congruent, more open to his experience, more realistic and effective in his ability to solve problems, less defensive and vulnerable and possessing a greater feeling of positive self-regard. Certain techniques, or characteristics of the counselor and counseling relationship, are directed toward achieving these aims throughout the seven stage process of the relationship.

a. *Acceptance.* The individual has become incongruent because conditions of worth have been attached to his concept of self. For congruence to occur, conditions of worth must be reduced. The therapist must provide an atmosphere of unconditionality for the client. He must accept the client without evaluating his fundamental worth or significance. The therapist, in fact, experiences *unconditional positive regard* for the client and has a prizing acceptance of him.

b. *Understanding.* The fundamental task of the counselor is to empathically understand the internal frame of reference of the individual, to experience the client's world of thoughts and feelings as if they were the therapist's own feelings. In this process of empathy, the counselor communicates a deep understanding to the client. *Reflection,* a technique of mirroring back in fresh words what the client has said or felt, may be employed for this reason. It is essential that the client feel he is both accepted and understood by the therapist.

c. *Congruence.* The counselor must be congruent in his relationship with the client. He must be non-contradictory and to some degree transparent. His feeling and attitude in the relationship is genuine and authentic. Where the counselor is perceived as incongruent by the client, the relationship is drastically inhibited, lacking in trust and openness.

B. Roy Grinker

Grinker's counseling model deals with the communication factors between individuals and is referred to as a *transactional approach*. The transaction involves all of the interrelationships of all *personal systems* in one's *field of experience*. The basis of counseling lies in the assumption that a client's transactions in therapy, and the roles and activities that these transactions include, represent the client's transactions in real life. They may be interpreted to the client, therefore, and in this process therapeutic benefit becomes manifest (Grinker, 1961).

V. EXISTENTIAL APPROACHES TO COUNSELING

Existential philosophy has increasingly influenced counseling theory in indirect and subtle ways. There are no single representatives of existentialist thought, and few commonly agreed upon first principles. Some basic concepts, however, are outlined by Patterson (1966), and their review provides a meaningful introduction to the existential system. His system is abstracted below (pp. 443–451).

A. Basic Concepts

1. *Man is distinguished from other beings in that he can become aware of his own existence; he is thus free and responsible for his existence.*
2. *Man exists in three separate worlds simultaneously.*
   a. *Umwelt*, the biological world having no self consciousness.
   b. *Mitwelt*, the world of human interactions in which reciprocal awareness is characteristic.
   c. *Eigenwelt*, the world of pure being, or self-identity.
3. *Man is dynamic and in flux; he is in a state of emergence or becoming.*
4. *As man is aware of being and existing, so too is he aware of nonbeing and nothingness. He may choose death at any moment.*

5. *Anxiety results in the struggle between being and nonbeing.*
   Existential anxiety is ultimately a threat to the individual's
   very existence.
6. *Each individual is unique and has his own world of self-iden-*
   tity (Eigenwelt). No two individuals are the same.
7. *Man, since he is a self-conscious being, has the capacity to*
   transcend himself. He is not identical with himself in the past.
8. *Modern man is described as alienated, depersonalized and*
   detached in the world. These are the presenting existential
   symptoms of the twentieth century.

B. Victor Frankl

One major proponent of the existential approach to psychotherapy and counseling is Victor Frankl. He sees man as a
whole entity existing in three dimensions, physical, mental and
spiritual. Traditional medical psychiatry deals with the first
two; the third dimension, the spiritual level, is the level of meaning and values. Frankl describes his approach to therapy as
logotherapy, a therapy of meaning to aid the individual with
philosophical, axiological and spiritual problems. The driving
force in the individual is not the will-to-power nor the will-to-
happiness, but the will-to-meaning in life. The major points of
concern for meaning center on the meaning of death, of life, of
work or of suffering and love. Problems here are *noogenic*
neuroses, spiritual difficulties involving existential frustration
over the failure to find meaning in one's world (Frankl, 1962).

The aim of logotherapy is to make man accept responsibility
for himself consciously and to help him find meaning in his life.

CHAPTER 14

COUNSELING II:
PROCESS AND TECHNIQUES

INTRODUCTION. When a counselor sees a client, he greets him, shakes his hand, perhaps, helps him to his chair, introduces him to the nature of counseling, and in one way or another, they begin an interaction which may have far-reaching consequences on the life of the client. Often the most important thing which happens to a client is when the counselor bids him goodbye and puts his arm on his shoulder as they go the the door.

In order to do *good* counseling, we wish to know what things work and what things do not. "Should I embrace all of my clients?" "Should I stop my client at the end of an hour, even if he's going strong?" "What should I say when he asks me how *I* feel about something?" These are questions of technique. While they seem simple, they are often extremely complex questions which cannot be answered by research or experience alone. Instead the counselor-trainee must attempt to understand what he does, to know what kinds of behavior he emits, i.e. what techniques he uses, and to learn new ways of relating to clients. Subsequently, he must somehow put his old behavior and new behavior together into some kind of a package which can function autonomously. When he can "sense" that it would be good to walk his client to the door with his arm on his shoulder so that this gesture is spontaneous and natural rather than a contrived therapeutic technique, then he is likely to be a facilitative counselor. In short, this chapter reviews some aspects of technique at the same time remembering that techniques alone or techniques as manipulative therapeutic devices are incomplete and often destructive counseling behaviors.

139

1. FACTORS AFFECTING COUNSELING

Certain situational variables and counselor characteristics affect the counseling relationship and determine its outcome. A review of these elements is preliminary to a discussion of techniques per se.

A. Setting

The physical arrangement of the counseling cubicle, its decor and furniture arrangement, the use of a desk, etc., may either help to facilitate an informal, warm and comfortable feeling for the client, or it may prove to be an obstacle to an easy flow of communication.

B. Privacy and Confidentiality

Essential to any effective counseling relationship is the feeling of confidence and trust on the part of the counselee. A room which is neither visually nor auditorally private implies nothing more than a superficial counseling encounter.

C. Tape Recording

Clients vary in their response or permission to record each session. A flexible and open arrangement between counselor and client can provide the best balance between the assurance of discretion for the client and the effective use of recordings for review, supervision and counselor-feedback purposes.

D. Counselor Beliefs and Values

The counselor does not engage in a relationship without his predispositions, beliefs and attitudes appearing in one form or another. Every counselor must recognize that his beliefs and values will play a role in *establishing the ethics in the relationship, shaping the goals of the relationship* (and therefore the outcomes) and *choosing the methods to be employed* in reaching those goals.

E. Counselor Acceptance and Understanding

A counselee who does not feel accepted and understood is not likely to experience much therapeutic progress. The communication of these abstract characteristics is highly complex and involves not only words but nonverbal attitudes as well.

F. Rapport, Attentiveness and Empathy

The degree to which the counselor-client relationship is characterized by a *bond of responsiveness and sensitivity* (*rapport*) and the degree to which the counselor is able to *feel into the client's world* (*empathy*) will determine to a large extent the levels of understanding the relationship will reach.

G. Congruence and Transparency

The counselor must be "seen through" in the sense that he is not wearing a facade of professionalism or that he is deliberately not going to express his feelings and values to a client under the guise of being nonevaluative and nonjudgemental. Some research evidence supports the notion that clients are facilitated by counselors who manifest qualities of *honesty, genuineness, openness* and *authenticity*. Congruency and transparency refer to this quality of the counselor being *whole* and *visible* to the client.

II. COUNSELING TECHNIQUES

Many of the techniques of counseling are tied to certain theories. Reflection, for example, is a method of dealing with a client which directly stems from client-centered theory; interpretation as a technique is anchored in psychoanalytic theory. In order to present an overview of counseling techniques, the theory to which it is allied, if any, is deliberately excluded in order to give the student more of a composite listing. Behavioral techniques are included in the chapter on counseling theories and are not repeated here.

A. Structuring

The way the counselor defines the nature, roles, goals and procedures to the client is called structuring the relationship. The effectiveness with which this is done may alleviate misconceptions or unreasonable expectations by the client at an early time.

1. *Amount of Structuring.*

When there are too many rules and limits imposed upon the relationship, it tends to become suffocated and lacking in spontaneity. On the other hand, when there is inadequate structuring, the client tends to respond to this ambiguous, undefined situation with insecurity, apprehensiveness and ultimately, defensiveness. Some minimal level of structuring which provides security and meaningfullness to the client, but which does not overburden the relationship is considered optimal.

2. *Types of Structure.*

Brammer and Shostram (1960) differentiate four types of structuring.

a. *Time limits.* The counselor may define the time aspects to the client in two ways: the expected length of each session and the approximate length of the entire counseling relationship.

b. *Action limits.* The counselor imposes limits on what clients may do behaviorally and what they may not do. A rule against destroying the office furniture would be an example.

c. *Role limits.* The role of the counselor must often be articulated to the client, e.g. that he is nonevaluative rather than a person in authority over the client, or that he is not an expert who provides advice but rather a person with whom the client works through his own problems.

d. *Process limits.* Process limits are conceptions about the nature of counseling and the counseling relationship which may be communicated verbally or nonverbally. While the client is usually free to discuss what he wishes, he gradually learns for example, that it is better to focus upon emotionally significant matters than it is to digress or intellectualize, or that going back into the past is of value in understanding the present only when such historical thinking does not detract from the intensity of the moment. These examples of process limits are developed by the client in interaction with the counselor, and their development may define the degree to which the relationship is meaningful and successful.

B. Leads

A lead is a term used to define the communications of the counselor as he interacts with the client's thinking. In one way or another, a lead *directs* some aspect of the client's thought process. The amount of leading, however, varies directly with the type of leads employed with the client. Various types of leads are described.

1. *Nondirective or Ambiguous Leads.*

A nondirective lead is one which poses a broad area of exploration for the client and which allows sufficient choice for the client to focus upon those feelings which he feels are most significant or puzzling. Example: "What is on your mind today?" or "Would you like to tell me more about that?"

2. *Directive Lead.*

This kind of lead is an evaluative communication, a judgment about the client's behavior; it implies what the client *ought to do.* Example: "Well why don't you seriously consider the possibility of dropping out of school!"

3. *Direct Question.*

Here the counselor places the client in a passive respondent position as he searches for specific answers to specific counselor-concerns.

4. *Reassurance.*

Any statement which is intended to imply sympathy or which attempts to pacify the client so that he *not feel so badly* or *not feel as he does* is a supportive lead by the counselor called reassurance. Example: "Don't worry, we're all like that!"

5. *Probing.*

When the counselor feels that the client ought to explore an area more thoroughly, or that there are underlying factors which ought to be uncovered, then the counselor is said to be probing. Example: "You say you feel inferior—if that is so, how does this feeling express itself in your sex life?"

6. *Confrontation.*

At times the counselor feels the client is being deliberately deceptive or is resisting the counseling process. When he directly addresses this deception or the client's previous contradictions, both verbal and nonverbal, he is confronting the client with material which the client has heretofore not faced. This is a delicate technique which may open up new areas in the relationship or it may simply act to polarize counselor and client, reinforcing a resisting pattern. Example: "You say you hate your father, but look at you—you're just about ready to cry!"

7. *Interpretation.*

Often the client's behavior remains partially unknown to him. Implications of what he says are sometimes easier for the counselor to see than for the client. When the counselor makes an analytic response which *goes beyond* the manifest content of the client's verbal or nonverbal behavior, he makes an interpretation. An interpretation may lead the client into deeper feeling levels and deeper levels of insight if it is timed appropriately and is at a level of depth which the client can still perceive. The disadvantage of interpretation is that it may convey distrust to the client, i.e. that the counselor is constantly looking for underlying meanings rather than just listening and accepting the client in a trusting way. Example: "You seem to have been saying in all of your sessions that you feel a need to hurt people—socially, on your job and at home. I wonder if you're not trying to prove something to yourself by all this."

C. Other types of Counselor Responses
1. *Silence.*

If properly structured and defined, silence may be a great value to the client. If his thinking wanders, he knows that he can follow his thoughts or feel into a problem without intervention or interruption by the counselor. Silence provides this space and allows this kind of exploration in an atmosphere of trust. It facilitates an opening of the relationship into deeper feeling levels if articulated appropriately.

2. *Reflection.*

Reflection is an attempt to put into fresh words the thoughts or feelings of the client. It is a kind of mirroring of the client by the counselor. Two types of reflection are distinguished; reflection of feeling, and reflection of content. In the first type the counselor focuses on the feelings expressed by the client and attempts to mirror them back, e.g. "You seem to be saying that you are really angry," even though some of the *content* of the client's message is missed or ignored. *Reflection of content* is where the basic facts and elements of the client's message are mirrored, almost summarized, but without an emphasis necessarily upon the feeling component. Reflection of content tends to be more cognitive and may provide some value to the client in terms of intellectual understanding and clarification of his thoughts, but it is not considered a technique designed to elicit feeling particularly. There are many difficulties with reflecting: the counselor may become stereotyped, his timing may be poor, he may be consistently selecting certain feelings over others or pursuing a level of depth which does not correspond to that of the client. However, when it is effected well, reflection allows the client to see himself and his feeling in a fresh way; it communicates the counselor's ability to understand and empathize, and it gives the client a kind of feedback he normally does not experience.

3. *Clarification.*

Responses which reorganize or synthesize what the client has said (content) or how he felt about what he said (feeling) are called clarifications. A clarification may be immediate, in that it follows directly after a client's response, or it may be a *summary clarification* which synthesizes what the client has said over a series of responses or an entire session.

4. *Forcing Client Responsibility.*

Many counseling models assume the client is responsible for change in therapy. The client seeks advice or external support rather than examining his own feelings. The counselor often reverses his communication to force the client into recognizing his role in the process. Example:

> CL: "What do you think I should do about my son?"
> C: "Well, what do *you* think you should do?"

5. *Acceptance.*

Any statements which indicate simple agreement and understanding, but do not imply approval or disapproval, are said to communicate acceptance. Example: 'M-hmm," "Yes, I see," etc.

6. *Persuasion, Cajoling and Attack.*

When the counselor wishes the client to engage in activities which he resists, the counselor may resort to very direct attack maneuvers. These techniques often produce *compliance* rather than real change in the client.

7. *Analyzing Communications.*

Certain patterns of counselee communications become important with time. Often the counselor observes them and tries to interpret them to the client. Some of these communication patterns are: *associational or conversational shifts, inconsistencies, recurrent remarks, concealed meanings, and gestures,* etc.

8. *Role Playing.*

The counselor may wish to have the client more clearly see a conflict with which he is dealing. He may ask the client to respond the way his mother or wife or child might respond, rather than to give the client's own response. Or the counselor may adopt a role, even the role of the client, while the client plays out another part. Role playing is used for a number of purposes and in a number of different ways. It is a delicate device which may improve understanding, empathy and communication as well as resolve unconscious and internal conflicts, when used effectively, and when the client reaches a point of readiness for the technique.

9. *Diagnosis and Interpretation.*

Another common counselor technique involves the systematic

observation of the client through appraisal instrumentation and the subsequent interpretation of this data to the client. The use of test data of this sort may adversely affect the counseling relationship if it seeks to remain nonjudgmental, permissive and open; on the other hand, it may provide useful information to the client so that he can appropriately plan a course of action or explore his own feelings in new ways.

III. STAGES OF COUNSELING

Various authors and theoreticians have conceptualized long and short term counseling as a gradual process which goes through definite stages or steps. It is impossible to treat all of these process-theories. Rather, the eight-stage process of Brammer and Shostram's Actualization counseling (1968, pp. 107–119) is cited as typical.

A. Step I: Awareness of the Need for Help

At this point the client achieves a readiness for counseling and makes certain basic assumptions about the counseling process. He is often aware of certain specific general problem areas, feelings of distress, etc.

B. Step II: Development of the Relationship and Overcoming Resistance

As counseling proceeds, the individual gradually senses the confidentiality and trust in the relationship, and earlier suspicious are overcome. This step is characterized as a relationship-building stage.

C. Step III: Expression of Feeling and Clarification of the Problems

Here the client, feeling trust in the therapist, expresses his feelings openly and ventilates or catharts many of the emotional pressures inside of him.

D. Steps IV and V: Exploration of Deeper Feelings and Awareness of Polarities

Often it is at stage IV and V that psychotherapy is distinguished from counseling. Here there is an increasing emphasis upon depth and a beginning confrontation with the basic core of personality. Deeper attitudes about self, the polarities in one's defensive adjustments and fundamental personality characteristics are addressed. Short term counseling may often not reach this level of activity.

E. Step VI: Working-Through and Integration Process

In steps IV and V, the client develops an awareness of his self-defeating, defensive and manipulative patterns. These characteristics are often well embedded in his personality, and the insight which he has developed is gradually broadened. This broadening of insight and increasing cognitive awareness is often a slow process of working-through old patterns and integrating insights into new behavioral approaches.

F. Step VII: Development of Awareness

This stage is characterized by an increased insightful awareness which began in Step VI. Here the emphasis is upon changed reactivity and changed patterns of response to previous conflicts. The individual broadens his awareness to grasp more global aspects of himself in the world.

G. Step VIII: Experience Outside Psychotherapy

In this stage the client begins to translate his insights and changed self-concepts into new behavior patterns, new relationships and generally new experiencing.

IV. SPECIAL RELATIONSHIP CHARACTERISTICS

Two characteristics of the counseling relationship which have not been mentioned are resistance and transference. These are phenomena which develop over time in the counselor-client interaction.

A. Resistance

Resistance refers to a client's conscious or unconscious attempt to deny or subvert progress or gain in therapy. There are various types of resistances and modes of dealing with it. Understanding resistance phenomena depends upon more lengthy reading into the interpersonal dynamics in counseling and psychotherapy. Generally, however, a client is said to be resisting when he consistently is late for his session, when he gets bored with himself and/or falls asleep, when he sets up games which he plays to avoid certain emotional realities, etc.

B. Transference

Transference refers to an irrational process in the client where he projects certain unresolved attitudes and roles upon the therapist. When the client becomes overly dependent upon counseling, as he might have done with his mother, or becomes antagonistic and suspicious of the therapist, as he might have done with his father, he is said to be transferring these childhood projections on to the counselor.

C. Countertransference

Countertransference is a term describing a reciprocal phenomena where the counselor himself becomes emotionally involved with his client and sees his client as a projection of his own emotional difficulties. Counseling effectiveness can be seriously undermined by an excessive countertransference.

COMMENTARY. Counseling techniques overlap each other. A question may be a probe, a nondirective lead, an interpretation or a host of other kinds of responses. Listing techniques, therefore, is a dubious method of classifying response patterns. Much depends upon the feeling tone and the contextual form of the particular response before one can assess what it is, and what effect it has.

CHAPTER **15**

GROUP COUNSELING

INTRODUCTION. Man is a social animal. Such problems as self-worth, alienation, loneliness, conformity, acceptance, prejudice and aggression are fundamentally rooted in the social context. A group utilizes this social context and as such, it can be a powerful and intense therapeutic medium in that it brings to bear forces which are not always found in individual counseling. Apart from being an economic means of treating many clients simultaneously, the group process marshalls such important interpersonal forces that it cannot be simply treated as a substitute for individual counseling. It is a legitimate and unique activity in its own right.

I. PURPOSES OF GROUPS

Purposes and objectives of group differs. Many different models for groups exist, and stated objectives tend to vary with the group model which is employed. Most group goals, however, would fit broadly within the following taxonomy.

A. Communication

Groups are organized to facilitate improved communication between individuals and subgroups.

B. Learning

Through sharing of experiences, group members may learn to improve their communication and relationship skills and learn to deal more effectively with their own feelings.

C. Insight

Groups are formed to increase awareness and self-understanding and to help members see into problems which they have hitherto disregarded or left unfinished.

D. Expression

A group may function as a specialized kind of laboratory where feelings which normally might be taboo in a conventional social context are allowed and ventilated in the group, providing an individual with a meaningful catharsis and release effect.

E. Orientation

A group may also be seen as an orienting device facilitating each member's readiness for individual counseling.

II. BASIC TERMINOLOGY

From the foundations of social psychology, sociology and communication theory, the study of groups has evolved into a complex network of terms, theories, empirical laws and clinical techniques. Some of the basic terminology is in need of clarification.

A. Group

The group is any aggregate of persons functioning together to achieve some mutual goal or objective.

B. Group Dynamics

The interacting forces within the group which facilitate or inhibit its movement are called group dynamics.

C. Group Process

Group process is the way the group functions to achieve its objectives and structure its identity. It is *how* the members act and interact together.

D. Group Therapy

Group therapy is the application of clinical principles and techniques on two or more individuals at the same time in order to correct or remediate specific psycho-social deficits and inadequacies.

E. Group Counseling

Group counseling is a relationship between a counselor and

two or more clients who engage in a social process which deals with factors concerning adjustment and development. Sometimes *multiple counseling* is used synonymously with group counseling in that it designates that there are many counselor-client relationships occurring at a given moment.

F. Group Guidance

Any activity or portion of the guidance program which is typified by participation of groups of students rather than by the individual counselor-client relationship is called group guidance.

III. TYPES AND MODELS OF GROUPS

A list of group types and models is difficult to exhaust. Some distinctions are more appropriate for sociology than counseling, others more relevant to clinical psychology and psychiatry than counseling. The name and label of the group, however, is perhaps less important than the orientation and techniques which may be implied by it. A survey of these styles of group activity, then, is of interest.

A. Primary and Secondary Groups

Originating in sociology, the primary group is a tight-knit structure with mutual interests (a family, for example) while a secondary group is any group not distinguished by such close contact.

B. Reference and Membership Groups

Similar to the distinction between primary and secondary groups, the reference group is characterized by some close identification of members with each other, while the membership group implies a more distant and formal sort of member identification.

C. In-group and Out-group

The in-group is homogeneous with respect to shared interests, values and characteristics, while the out-group is seen as heterogeneous and different.

D. Psyche- and Socio-groups

A psyche-group is one in which membership is based on psychological and emotional need satisfaction, while socio-groups are predisposed toward external goals.

E. Continuous and Closed Groups

A group may be continuous if membership may be obtained at any time. If membership and participation are dictated from the beginning with no new participants, the group is a closed group.

F. Didactic Groups

A group which is organized around a group leader who presents educationally oriented material for discussion is termed didactic.

G. Therapeutic Social Groups

Used often in a mental hospital setting, the therapeutic social group is organized in order to increase skills in social participation and activity.

H. Inspirational Groups

A group which emphasizes strong mutual identification of members and stresses positive elements is an inspirational group. Alcoholics Anonymous would be such an example.

I. Psychodramatic Groups

The use of psychodrama techniques has grown in recent years. The psychodramatic group is one in which members act out each other's problems in various ways in order to clairfy, delineate and understand particular internal or external role conflicts.

J. Free-interaction Groups

Most typically used in group therapy situations, free-interaction groups are those which attempt to elicit expression of deeply felt concerns and feelings from the members without any formalized agenda.

K. T-groups

A T-group or training-group is one having no stated roles or goals. The ambiguity of the situation is thought to create a setting for minor identity-crises in the group members, and the group operates as a laboratory for interpersonal learning.

L. Developmental Groups

Groups which are organized around the growth and development of members and characterized by mutual purposes, flexible organization and positive social control and leadership are termed developmental groups.

M. Marathon Groups

A marathon group is a continuous group which may last from fourteen to forty-eight hours. Members must remain in the group at all times. Routine therapeutic procedures, techniques or games are usually eliminated and more attention focused upon the massing of immediate feelings and tensions which accumulate the longer the group is in session. The high levels of intensity which are reached make the marathon a unique group medium for psychotherapeutic gain and improved emotional effectiveness with self and others. The marathon group usually is made up of about twelve members.

N. Group Behavior Modification

Following principles of operant conditioning, a behavorial group is characterized as a learning medium. Members define and stipulate their own difficulties and establish their own learning outcomes. Each member then attempts to reinforce particular behavioral sequences which the other group member wants to either increase or extinguish. Activity outside the group to achieve these learning outcomes is also heavily emphasized.

O. Family Therapy; Conjoint Family Groups

Rather than doing individual therapy with one or another

family member, an entire family may be organized in a group to achieve a mutual and reciprocal level of responsibility for change in all members. It is a direct and often more intense activity than counseling family members separately.

IV. GROUP AND INDIVIDUAL COUNSELING: SIMILARITIES AND DIFFERENCES

The counselor is engaged in both individual and group counseling. It is essential that his experience lead him to a fuller understanding of the two counseling methodologies in order to utilize each most effectively with the variety of clients he will meet.

A. Similarities

1. *Common Objectives.*

In terms of helping the client to achieve greater self-integration and responsibility, both methods share common objectives.

2. *Permissive Climate.*

Usually both methods maintain a permissive and open climate in order to facilitate the client's achievements of greater understanding and expression.

3. *Counselor Technique Important.*

The orientation and technique of the counselor does not substantially change from the individual to the group situation. In both, the behavior of the counselor is essential to the progress of the client or clients.

4. *Privacy and Confidentiality.*

The assurance of discretion in communication is common to both types of counseling. In the group, however, all members are bound by the rule, not just the counselor.

B. Differences

1. *Peer Interaction.*

The group situation provides the client an atmosphere of

immediate feedback from his peers. In this respect group counseling is more of a social learning milieu than individual counseling.

2. *Multiple Helping Relationships.*

The resources and potential help offered to a client increases as the number of members increases. This is not always the case, however, and depends largely on the similarity of member needs, the cohesiveness of the group, and other interaction variables.

3. *Increased Couselor Role.*

In the group the counselor must be aware of more variables than the one-to-one relationship. He must try to become aware of and understand not only the counselor-client interaction but client-client factors operating in the group.

V. BASIC PRINCIPLES OF GROUP COUNSELING

It is obvious that different counseling orientations and different models of groups will follow different principles of organization. Some general principles of group counseling, however, are relevant to school counseling and in some degree, independent of theory and orientation of the individual counselor.

A. **Group counseling does not necessarily substitute for individual counseling**

B. **The group can have a significant impact on member attitudes, values and personality traits**

C. **The effectiveness of a group depends largely on its mutuality of purpose, commitment from its members and its cohesiveness**

VI. GROUP STRUCTURE

The organization and structure of groups may be looked at from a number of respects. The basic elements of group structure may be applied in the analysis of any type of group model. The structure of every group is determined by how it operates (process) and what it is concerned with (content).

A. Process

Whether a group is successful in meeting its objectives or whether it fails is determined by how it operates and what procedures and methods it uses in attempting to reach these goals.

1. *Formation.*

One means of analyzing the process of a group is to determine how it came into being, whether membership was voluntary or required, formal or informal. Depending on the type of formation, the group may be successful or unsuccessful.

2. *Membership and Leadership.*

The style of group leadership may have positive and negative effects on its functioning. Types of leadership styles and leader behavior have been described in group process research.

a. *Some Leadership Styles*

    (1) Authoritarian.
    (2) Democratic.
        (a) Participatory.
        (b) Consultative.
        (c) Supervisory.
    (3) Laissez-faire.
    (4) Other Types.
        (a) Charismatic.
        (b) Bureaucratic.

b. *Some Leader Behaviors* (Brammer and Shostram, 1968)

    (1) Moderating.
    (2) Problem setting.
    (3) Idea developing.
    (4) Amending.
    (5) Initiating.

    (6) Supporting.
    (7) Opposing.
    (8) Summarizing.
    (9) Controlling.
    (10) Sentiment-testing.
    (11) Energizing.

3. *Communication and Perception.*

Different clients see and react to other client-members with varying words having varying meanings. The *way* the group communicates and perceives contributes to understanding its process and style.

4. *Problem-solving Behavior.*

Groups meet expected and unexpected problems while in process. The *way* these problems and the resultant frustrations and reactions are resolved play a large role in determining the prognosis of the group and in characterizing its style.

B. Content

The group content is simply what the group is all about. The content of most groups is some form of personal-social counseling. On the other hand, groups in schools may be organized around other kinds of content.

1. *Orientation and Articulation.*

Group procedures have often been used to articulate program information to prospective students and to help orient them to the school, prevailing student attitudes and codes, etc. The group procedures here may take the form of college days, freshman weeks, courses on orientation or small group arrangements with guidance staff or student leaders serving as coordinators.

2. *Student Activities.*

The effective utilization of group procedures in orientation and articulation can be adapted to the variety of student activities particularly those involving autonomous or leaderless groups.

3. *Interpreting Test Data.*

Frequently the interpretation of test results is cumbersome in the individual counseling situation in that not all students interested can be served by such a technique, and also the test data may, under certain circumstances, inhibit other counselor-client relationship variables. Group activities, therefore, have fruitfully been used to discuss psychological test interpretation, the nature of norms, measurement principles, etc.

4. *Educational Planning.*

Groups of students or parents having similar interests in planning appropriate educational experiences may profit from group activities by learning from each other and the counselor of educational opportunities, curricular options and sometimes the more fundamental problems of establishing realistic levels of educational aspiration, etc.

5. *Occupational Planning.*

Occupational and vocational development has received greater emphasis in the school guidance process. Choosing an occupation is less seen as a single event, but as a gradual and developmental career-selection process of enormous complexity. Planning such groups along a developmental model is a new facet of many guidance programs. A vocational development group may continue for some time, get involved in the organization of work-study activities and often develop provisions for on-the-job training experiences for its members.

7. *Organized Guidance Courses.*

The group guidance course approach has had a difficult history. Without mutual and relatively homogeneous interests, group guidance courses may be unsuccessful. Properly programmed, however, occupations courses, homeroom programs and other guidance classes or courses may be exceptional learning experiences.

VII. THE GROUP COUNSELING PROCESS

Group counseling is a kind of facilitating activity emphasizing growth and interpersonal development with essentially normal clients. It is a dynamic process which may occur in school or in other settings and which may stay at a problem-centered or adjustment level, or it may reach deeper levels of feeling encounters. Some general considerations are worth noting about group counseling processes.

A. Selecting and Excluding Clients

Since the group is not psychotherapeutic or remedial, it begins at a point of relative adjustment in its members and moves *forward* towards increasing growth and expanding one's interpersonal skills and awareness. Certain screening activities may be necessary, therefore, to establish how disturbed some clients may be. Most sources feel three general behavior patterns or types of clients ought be excluded from group counseling.

1. *Clients with poor reality contact.*
2. *Clients with psychopathic defenses and behavior patterns.*
3. *Clients with excessive monopolizing tendencies.*

B. Initiating Procedures

Four basic factors should be effectively addressed before the group goes very far.

1. *Structuring Goals and Purposes.*

Some explanation and articulation of what counseling is about, what the group is for, where members hope to go with it, etc., should be looked at early in the first session or before.

2. *Maintaining Workable Group Size.*

Effective group formations usually range between six to ten members. A workable size, as well as a rule governing the entrance of new members, if any, is necessary.

3. *Length and Frequency of Sessions.*

It is recommended that a group meet approximately weekly, though this may vary from twice weekly to once every two weeks. Sessions for elementary children range from thirty to forty minutes, for adolescents from one to one and one-half hours and for adults from one and one-half to two hours.

4. *Establishing Discretion and Confidentiality.*

The rule of confidentiality must be established from the outset of the group. Trust and intimacy may be seriously hampered without a clear statement of this rule in the initial session.

C. Phases of Group Counseling

Attempts have been made to document the stages a group goes through. Not every group goes lock-step through these levels, but some idea of how groups function over a series of sessions is of value. Not each step abstracted below is achieved in a single session, but may be spread over a number of meetings.

1. *Step I: Establishment of rapport and some emotional release.*
2. *Step II: Exploration, listening and acceptance of member attitudes.*
3. *Step III: Growing individual and group understanding and awareness.*
4. *Step IV: Increasing problem-solving skills and self-concept changes.*
5. *Step V: Acceptance of termination and evaluation of the group.*

D. Techniques of Group Counseling

Many techniques in individual counseling may be used in a group setting. Reflection and clarification would be such examples. There are some techniques unique to group work, however, and these are listed here.

1. *"Going Around."*

In order to warm up the group and to achieve some direct feeling contact between members rather than remain content-oriented or intellectualized, the group leader may ask each member of the group to give his or her first impressions or significant emotional feelings toward all the other members of the group.

2. *Structuring.*

The counselor attempts to define the nature and goals of the group initially. As the group proceeds, however, he asserts other kinds of goals or process rules, e.g. that members should address each other in the first person rather than the third, or that when one member is addressing another, he should look him in the eye, rather than looking elsewhere. These kinds of process rules emerge in the group and promote deeper and more effective open communication.

3. *Psychodramatic Techniques.*

Psychodrama is a highly systematized form of group psychotherapy deserving of much further attention by the student interested in group work. Many of the techniques of psychodrama have been utilized within a more traditional group counseling model. Some of these are listed.

a. *Role Reversal.* Where two members appear to have difficulty communicating and understanding each other's respective position, they may be asked to take each other's role in the group, e.g. a black man takes on the role of the white man and vice versa.

b. *Alter Ego.* Here another individual attempts to take on the role of the client and attempts to express those thoughts that he feels the client has not expressed.

c. *Mute Technique.* The mute technique involves acting out scenes and communicating nonverbally using only gestures.

d. *Awareness and Expression of Polarities.* When individuals have strong ambivalent feelings, they are often asked to express both sides of the conflict and to focus upon both extremes of feeling. A man with both masculine and feminine tendencies may be asked to have his masculine side communicate with his feminine side and to develop this internal dialogue in the group.

4. *Summary Interpretation.*

Sometimes the group leader may attempt to terminate a session by summarizing or interpreting the major emotionally significant themes in the group process or may make an individual analysis of each participant's movement during the group. A co-therapist may also assume this function at the end of the group session.

5. *Other Techniques.*

The growth of sensitivity training and gestalt therapy has brought numerous kinds of exercises and techniques designed to provoke intensive bodily, self or interpersonal awareness. These techniques cannot be used effectively in isolation but depend upon the development of an integrated "agenda" and a specially trained group leader. A partial list of some of these techniques is given here. Further elaboration of these and other awareness exercises is given in the literature (Shutz, 1967).

a. *Relaxation exercises.*
b. *Blind walk.*
c. *Trust fall.*
d. *Back lift.*
e. *Doubling.*
f. *Free association.*
g. *Alone time.*
h. *Guided fantasy.*
i. *Break-in.*
j. *Milling.*
k. *Group fantasy.*
l. *Physical confrontation.*
m. *Pushing.*
n. *Breaking out.*
o. *Video tape feedback.*

COMMENTARY: A group is not always within the therapeutic control of the counselor. Sometimes it is bigger than he is. Often, it ought to be. His role may need to diminish, and he may have to become a participant with the group. The spontaneity and wealth of interaction between members of the group may reach such levels of productive dynamism and intensity that the counselor role is momentarily unnecessary; the interactions that are taking place are themselves facilitating.

On the other hand, this quality of emergence and dynamism in the group has destructive elements, particularly where interactions are operating at a high level and individuals with premorbid personalities succumb or distort experiences to such a degree that the group no longer can facilitate or rectify what has happened. It is at this time that individual follow-up is necessary by the responsible counselor to work through these serious distortions with the client and to help him reestablish his personality integrity and coping mechanisms. Effective screening might have prevented this episode, but any counselor who does extensive group work must be prepared for these eventualities, even when screening devices are employed.

CHAPTER 16

APPRAISAL I:
TESTS AND MEASUREMENTS

INTRODUCTION TO APPRAISAL. Recognizing that individuals are both similar and different, the scope of the inventory or assessment service is to focus on the individuality of each pupil, to gather meaningful information about him and his environment and, in this process, to aid him in understanding himself, and to make effective decisions from this understanding.

I. TEST TECHNIQUES OF APPRAISAL

Testing is a more specific term than appraisal in that it implies some form of standardized instrument or battery of instruments which measure some limited characteristic or trait of an individual. Appraisal refers to any systematic means of gathering information about a pupil. Testing is, therefore, only one appraisal technique.

A. Purpose of Tests

Teachers, counselors, psychologists and administrators may use tests for different purposes.

1. *Prediction.*

Tests are often used to estimate how well an individual will do at some later time.

2. *Prediction.*

Often counselors use tests to aid the client in anticipating how well he may be able to perform in various academic or occupational roles at some later time.

3. *Decision-making.*

Tests may be used to facilitate planning educational or vocational careers, choosing activities which correspond to tested interests or changing college majors as a result of aptitude and interest profiles.

4. *Diagnosis.*

Tests may enable the counselor to better understand factors in maladjustment or educational inadequacy.

5. *Evaluation.*

The counselor may use assessment techniques to judge the progress of counseling decisions, or to evaluate the effectiveness of the entire counseling service.

B. Ways of Classifying Tests

Usually tests are discussed in terms of their function (ability, aptitude, etc.). However, tests may be classified according to their content, procedure or other factors (Schertzer & Stone, 1966).

1. *Standardized Versus Teacher-made Tests.*

Standardized tests are those which follow specific instructions for administration and scoring. Teacher-made tests are usually less formal and are constructed for evaluation within the classroom.

2. *Individual Versus Group Tests.*

Individual tests are usually administered by a trained examiner while group tests can be administered to more than one pupil at a time.

3. *Speed Versus Power Tests.*

Speed tests depend on completing a series of items within a specific time limit. Power tests attempt to measure the scope and depth of a person's knowledge.

4. *Performance Versus Paper-and-pencil Tests.*

Typically performance tests involve the manipulation of objects, solving puzzles, etc., while paper and pencil tests require only marks on an answer sheet.

5. *Maximum Versus Typical Performance Tests.*

A maximum performance test requires the individual to perform at his best, whereas a typical performance test tries to determine what an individual usually does.

C. Characteristics of Adequate Tests

Counselors and other school professionals use certain general criteria to tell if one test is more suited to their purpose than another.

1. *Appropriate Norms.*

A norm is a numerical value which describes the performance of various groups on a test inventory. Norms provide a basis for comparing scores.

2. *Standardization.*

The provision for fixed procedures in administering and scoring the tests as well as the establishment of suitable age, grade and sex norms is generally characteristic of standardized tests.

3. *Reliability.*

Reliability is the consistency or accuracy of measurement. A test is reliable to the degree that it consistently produces similar results. Reliability is expressed numerically in terms of a coefficient of correlation. Reliability is expressed as a value ranging from 0.00 to +1.00. An acceptable minimum coefficient for a standardized test would probably be +.70. However, there are different types of reliability coefficients.

a. *Test-Retest Reliability Coefficient.* The most frequently used measure of reliability, this coefficient is obtained by comparing two sets of scores on tests which have been administered to a group on one occasion, then readministered on another. The higher the reliability coefficient between the scores obtained on each occasion, the more likely it is that the test is consistent in its measurement of the trait it purports to measure.

b. *Split-Half Reliability Coefficient.* This coefficient is obtained by partitioning the test into two sets of scores in which the partition of the test is made either on the basis of odd versus even numbered items or by splitting the test into two halves (e.g. items 1–10 are correlated to items 11–20).

c. *Parallel-Form Reliability Coefficient.* This coefficient is obtained by comparing two sets of scores derived from two forms of the same test.

4. *Validity.*

Validity is the extent to which a test does what it is meant to do. Certain types of validity are expressed numerically while others are not.

a. *Criterion-related Validity.* When a test correlates with some external criterion which is said to be related to the test itself, some measure of criterion-related validity may be determined. If, for example, a teacher wishes to know if her arithematic achievement test is valid, she may compare her results on this test with the school wide standardized achievement test and compute a correlation coefficient. If the coefficient is high, she may be confident that her test and the school wide achievement test are measuring similar things and, therefore, that her test is valid.

(1) *Predictive Validity.* One form of criterion-related validity is obtained when the test is correlated with some criterion measure *given at some later time.*

(2) *Concurrent Validity.* When the criterion measure is collected *at the same time* as the test, a measure of concurrent validity is obtained.

b. *Content Validity.* This type of validity is sometimes called *rational* or *logical* validity and is not expressed numerically, nor is it related to an external criterion. It is brought about by seeing that the test covers the intended content or sample of behavior appropriately. A test of "general achievement" for example, which covers spelling exhaustively but does not treat mathematics at all, does not cover the area of "general achievement" appropriately and would have low content validity.

c. *Construct Validity.* Construct validity tells us whether the test is meaningful theoretically and is usually determined by investigating what psychological traits or factors a test measures. A number of techniques may be used to assess it.

5. *Other Factors.*

Apart from these traditional criteria for judging the suitability of a particular test, practical concerns also come to bear. The examiner must select a test knowing whether the *age norms* incorporate the population or class he wishes to test, whether the class has had *previous experience* taking the test, how much *time* will be necessary for administration and scoring, etc.

II. TYPES OF TESTS

A. Mental Ability Tests

Also termed intelligence, academic ability or scholastic aptitude tests, mental ability tests attempt to estimate the intellectual functioning of an individual. Measurement of human intelligence, however, depends largely on the definition of intelligence which is used.

1. *Definitions of Intelligence.*

a. *L. M. Terman.* Largely responsible for adapting the Binet-Simon test to America and creating the Stanford Binet, Terman defined intelligence as simply *"the ability to think in terms of abstract ideas"* (Terman & Merrill, 1937, p. 3).

b. *David Wechsler.* Creator of the second most widely used individual intelligence tests, Wechsler defined intelligence as *"the aggregate of global capacity of the individual to think rationally, and to deal effectively with his environment"* (1958, p. 7).

2. *History of Ability Testing.*

Mental ability tests were the first systematic psychological tests to be developed.

a. *Wilhelm Wundt.* Establishing the first psychological laboratory in Leipzig, Wundt studied man's intelligence through measures of reaction time.

b. *James McKeen Cattell.* Cattell received his Ph.D. from Wundt and brought to America the study of individual differences in intelligence through measures of motor and sensory performance.

c. *Alfred Binet and Theodore Simon.* Together they published the first intelligence scale (1905–1911). The test was designed to separate underachievers from the feeble-minded in Paris schools.

d. *L. M. Terman.* Terman revised the Binet-Simon scale and through subsequent revisions and restandardizations, helped to produce the most contemporary version of the original scale: The Stanford Binet 1960 Form LM.

e. *World War I.* American psychologists led by A. S. Otis and Robert Yerkes were assigned the task of developing accurate mental screening tests for the army. These efforts resulted in the Army Alpha and Army Beta tests.

f. *L. L. Thurstone.* Using factorial methods, Thurstone devised an intelligence test in the 1930s based on what he termed primary mental abilities.

g. *David Wechsler.* In the late thirties Wechsler developed an adult intelligence test, the Wechsler-Bellevue. A decade later the Wechsler Adult Intelligence Scale (WAIS) appeared and subsequently, the Wechsler Intelligence Scale for Children (WISC).

h. *World War II.* The second world war brought increased emphasis on screening and selection tests to be used with draftees and resulted in the Army General Classification Test (AGCT).

3. *Theories of Intelligence.*

Since many definitions of intelligence have been used to create the variety of measures of intelligence, it may be supposed that many theories of intelligence underlie these efforts. In many cases these theories overlap each other when put to use.

a. *Unifactor Theory.* The assumption here is that intelligence is an aggregate phenomena not specific to any single abilities.

b. *Two-factor Theory.* The two-factor theory, most commonly traced to *Charles Spearman* holds that intelligence is composed of a general capacity factor ("g" factor) and factors specific to given tasks ("s" factor).

c. *Multiple Factor Theory.* Intelligence is made up of a number of specific abilities. *Thurstone's* primary mental abilities and *J. P. Guilford's* notions on the structure of the intellect fall in this grouping.

4. *Abuse of the IQ Concept.*

An IQ of 130 is meaningless, and by itself is neither good nor bad. If the IQ of 130 is derived from an unreliable test or one which has poor validity, it is certainly dissimilar to an IQ of 130 derived from a test which is reliable and valid. Furthermore, IQ scores by themselves may represent different percentiles, and on Test X the IQ of 130 represents the ninety-second percentile while on Test Y it represents the sixty-third percentile. The lack of equivalency from test to test makes the IQ only meaningful if it is related to the specific distribution of IQ's provided by the test manual. (Specific treatment of intelligence quotients and their relation to mental ability and retardation is given in the chapter on *Mental Retardation, Learning Disabilities and Underachievement*).

5. *Types of Ability Tests.*

Intelligence tests may be grouped in terms of those requiring individual administration by a trained examiner versus those which can be administered to groups. The most frequently used tests are listed below.

a. *Individual Tests.*

  (1) Stanford-Binet Intelligence Scale, Form LM.
  (2) Wechsler Adult Intelligence Scale (WAIS).
  (3) Wechsler Intelligence Scale for Children (WISC).
  (4) Goodenough Draw-A-Man Test.
  (5) Peabody Picture Vocabulary.

b. *Group Tests.*

  (1) California Test of Mental Maturity.
  (2) Otis Quick Scoring Mental Ability Tests.

(3) SRA Primary Mental Abilities Test.

(4) Lorge-Thorndike Intelligence Tests.

c. *The WISC: An Example.* Most school counselors are not trained to administer individual intelligence tests like the Wechsler Intelligence Scale for Children (WISC), although many are increasingly being trained. This test is one of the two most widely used clinical instruments for IQ assessment, and if a school counselor is to function collaboratively with school psychologists or other pupil personnel specialists, he is certain to encounter many a diagnostic report which includes WISC results.

(1) *Type of test.* The WISC is an individually administered, standardized test for children from ages 5 to 15. It takes about 60 minutes to administer. The test is reliable and has good validity coefficients. Its standardization is also quite expansive.

(2) *Scales.* Intelligence is conceived as an aggregate or global capacity. The test provides a global IQ score, called the *full-scale* IQ. It is made up of two major subfunctions: verbal and performance, each having its own subscales. The verbal IQ is made up of subtests such as *Information, Comprehension, Arithmetic, Digit Span, Similarities* and *Vocabulary.* Performance IQ is drawn from the subtests *Picture Arrangement, Picture Completion, Block design, Object Assembly, Digit Symbol* and/or *Mazes.* The combined Verbal and Performance IQs yield the Full Scale IQ.

(3) *Uses.* The WISC is not only a device which is used to classify children on the basis of an IQ score, the analysis of subtests scores and patterns is of tremendous diagnostic value in assessing certain intellectual deficits, making curricular recommendations, detecting perceptual and organic difficulties, etc. Such analysis, however, depends upon skilled interpretation.

B. Achievement Tests

Achievement tests attempt to measure the performance of a pupil within the context of his subject matter. They may be defined as instruments measuring the results of instruction.

Achievement tests measure proficiency in a series of areas (Schertzer & Stone, 1966).

1. *Types of Achievement Tests.*

a. *Survey Tests.* These achievement tests typically assess the pupil's proficiency in broad areas of subject matter and provide a basis for comparing pupils in their relative standing with other pupils within each subject area and across all subjects.

b. *Readiness and Prognostic Tests.* A test which attempts to predict whether an individual can profit from additional training or how well he can be expected to perform at a higher level of instruction is called a readiness or prognostic test.

c. *Diagnostic Tests.* Tests of achievement which are designed to assist teachers and counselors in spotting areas of weakness and strength with specific academic abilities, e.g. reading, arithmetic, language skills, are termed diagnostic tests.

2. *History of Achievement Tests.*

a. *Horace Mann.* An outstanding educator, Mann first employed written achievement examinations in Boston in the 1840s.

b. *New York State Regents Examinations.* Stemming from Mann's influence, written examinations were used in New York State in 1865.

c. *Joseph Meyer Rice.* In 1897 Rice reported a study on spelling achievement. Over 29,000 children were tested, and norms were presented.

d. *College Entrance Examinations.* In 1900 the College Boards were first given.

e. *R. B. Tyler and E. G. Green.* These two investigators conducted an eight year study on retention, using achievement tests. Their study raised the issue of whether achievement tests should be exclusively concentrated on the assessment of knowledge for facts, since such great proportions of facts were not retained after instruction was completed.

3. *Standardized Group Achievement Tests.*

a. *California Achievement Tests.*
b. *Stanford Achievement Tests.*

c. *Iowa Tests of Basic Skills.*
d. *Durrell Analysis of Reading Difficulty.*
e. *Sequential Tests of Educational Progress.*
f. *Metropolitan Achievement Tests.*

C.   Aptitude Tests

Aptitude is frequently confused with achievement or ability. While there is some overlap between these areas, aptitudes are generally thought to be certain underlying capacities of individuals in specific areas. Aptitudes predict future achievement.

1. *History of Aptitude Tests.*

a. *Carl E. Seashore.* One of the first aptitude tests of musical talent was developed by Seashore and remains in use today.

b. *World War II.* The influx of servicemen during the war required screening batteries which would assess aptitudes in numerous areas upon which effective decisions could be made for placement and training of draftees.

c. *Factor Analysis.* The advent of factor analysis led to the construction of multi-factor batteries which could refine the dimensions and variables in aptitude tests.

2. *Types of Aptitude Tests.*

Large numbers of aptitude tests are employed in education and industry assessing specific aptitudes, e.g. clerical aptitude or general groups of aptitudes as in the multi-factor batteries.

a. *Differential Aptitude Test.*
b. *General Aptitude Test Battery.*
c. *Guilford-Zimmerman Aptitude Survey.*
d. *Minnesota Clerical Test.*
e. *Seashore Measures of Musical Talents.*
f. *Aptitude Tests for Occupations.*

D.   Interest Inventories

Interests are defined as the pupil's curiosity or intentness about some object. Interest inventories are frequently used by counselors and teachers in learning about a child's likes or dislikes and in helping the client in counseling to see in a systematic fashion a profile of his vocational and/or educational interest patterns.

1. *History of Interest Inventories.*

Not only have interest inventories been of use, historically, to counselors and teachers, but they have been widely used by business and industry in the proper utilization of personnel.

a. *E. K. Strong.* Strong developed one of the first vocational interest inventories. The inventory sampled likes and dislikes and correlated these responses with interests of persons employed in differing occupations.

b. *L. L. Thurstone.* Using factor analytic methods, Thurstone took eighteen scales of the Strong Vocational Interest Blank and helped to refine the subsequent construction of interest inventories.

2. *Types of Interest Inventories.*

The most prominent and widely used interest measures are the Strong Vocational Interest Blank (SVIB) and the Kuder Preference Record. Since these are instruments often used by counselors, some detailed description of each is essential.

a. *Strong Vocational Interest Blank.* This interest inventory was developed by Edward K. Strong and is made up of some 400 items which the individual responds to by indicating L (like), I (Indifferent) or D (Dislike). Items are concerned with occupations, school subjects, amusements, activities and types of people. There are separate forms for men and women. Norms for men are based upon extensive research with different occupational groups having common likes and dislikes which distinguish them from men in general. The client's interest patterns are compared to these various occupational groups, e.g. artists, psychologists, lawyers and mathematicians. The SVIB has some fifty such occupational areas on the male forms and twenty-six for women. The scores obtained allow the client to rate his interests in relation to the interest of persons in these specific jobs, to find which occupations his interest patterns are similar to and to which occupations his interest patterns are dissimilar. The inventory is easy to administer and is scored by the test publisher.

b. *Kuder Preference Record.* Developed by G. F. Kuder using factor analytic techniques to identify clusters of interests, the Kuder is made up of several forms, vocational, personal and occupational. Items are of a forced-choice variety. Each item has three alternatives. The client selects the one he likes most and the one he likes least, leaving the third item blank. Raw scores are converted to percentiles, and norms are provided for males and females at high school and adult levels. Certain interests cluster together to form patterns. On the Vocational form, for example, interest may point to the following major cluster areas: mechanical, outdoor, computational, scientific, persuasive, artistic, literary, musical, social service or clerical. From these interest groups, many occupational possibilities may be explored with the client, i.e. occupations which belong to these particular interest clusters.

3. *Problems with Interest Inventories.*

Interests are dependent on many factors. Interests can change with age, under certain conditions of testing and with the nature of the testing instrument. Some of these problems must be appraised by the person who interprets the interest profile.

a. *Answers can easily be faked.*

b. *Vocubulary and reading level may be too high.*

c. *Socially acceptable choices may predominate over true feelings.*

E. Personality Inventories

There are many types of personality theories, definitions of personality and concepts of what goes into making a mature personality. There are just as many, if not more, varieties of assessment techniques and tests in the measurement of personality.

1. *History of Personality Tests.*

a. *Kraeplin.* One of the earliest devices for screening emotionally disturbed patients was a free association measure designed by Kraeplin. *Carl Jung* later worked in this area using a word association list.

b. *Robert Woodworth.* During World War I, Woodworth developed the Personal Data Sheet, a prototype of later personality tests, which attempted to screen out seriously disturbed men from the military services.

2. *Types of Personality Tests.*

While many approaches exist for personality assessment, some are more appropriate for the counselor than others.

a. *Free Association Technique.* Used primarily by psychoanalytic therapists, this technique requires the patient to speak out the first things which enter his mind. The therapist attempts to relate his response to various diagnostic criteria.

b. *Situational Tests.* The client in these performance-type tests performs a task in simulated everyday situations, and his responses are systematically observed.

c. *Projective Techniques.* By providing an ambiguous stimulus to a client, e.g. an ink blot, an ill-defined picture or an incomplete sentence, the client will respond to these items and unwittingly reveal something of himself.

d. *Personality Questionnaire.* The most common assessment device is the self-reporting paper-and-pencil test which has been standardized with representative groups of normals and emotionally disturbed individuals.

3. *Specific Personality Tests.*

More than any other type of test, personality tests suffer most from the problems of adequate reliability and validity. Caution is essential in selecting a personality test appropriate for use by the counselor or for the school testing program.

a. *Projective Tests.* Most, if not all, major projective devices are individually administered by trained examiners.

(1) *Blacky Pictures.*
(2) *Children's Apperception Test.*
(3) *Draw-A-Person Test.*
(4) *Rorschach Test.*
(5) *Thematic Apperception Test.*

b. *Paper-and-Pencil Tests.* Because of their usual standardization and provision for norms, these tests are more frequently
used by practicing counselors.

(1) *Minnesota Multiphasic Personality Inventory* (MMPI).

(2) *Bell Adjustment Inventory.*

(3) *California Test of Personality.*

(4) *Edwards Personal Preference Schedule.*

(5) *Mooney Problem Checklist.*

c. *The MMPI: An example.* Certainly one of the most widely
used and widely researched paper-and-pencil personality tests
is the *Minnesota Multiphasic Personality Inventory.* It is, perhaps, less often used in schools than in other settings by counseling psychologists. It is, however, one of the most extensive
measures of personality and psychopathology for individuals
sixteen and older. The MMPI is made up of some 550 statements
which the client must answer either "true," "false" or "cannot
say." The items refer to different types of psychopathology. The
550 items fall into various groupings or scales (Anastasi, 1968).

(1) *The Nine Major Scales.*

(a) *Hypochondriasis;* a measure of one's overconcern
with bodily functions and general health.

(b) *Depression;* a measure of one's tendency to be
despondent or depressed.

(c) *Hysteria;* a measure of one's loss of movement or
tendency to develop physical symptoms without the presence of physical causes.

(d) *Paranoia;* a measure of one's tendency to be overly
suspicious of others.

(e) *Masculinity-Femininity;* a measure of one's display
of male versus female behavioral characteristics.

(f) *Hypomania;* a measure of excessive physical and
mental activity in relation to elation and ecstacy.

(g) *Schizophrenia;* a measure of one's tendency to
withdraw from social activity with evident eccentricities
in behavior.

(h) *Psychasthenia;* a measure of obsessive and compulsive tendencies.

(i) *Psychopathic*; a measure of one's disregard for social sanctions and general ethical standards of conduct.

(2) *Other factors.* The MMPI also uses supplemental scales, e.g. the Lie scale, the K scale, the F scale, etc., which measure the degree to which a person answers consistently, how defensive he appears to be in answering the test questions, and other so-called "response sets." The MMPI provides a profile of results for each of the major and supplemental scales and allow the clinician to interpret quantitatively which scores are within a normal range and which scores or combination of scores indicate neurotic or psychotic patterns. Many controversies have emerged with the use of the MMPI such as whether certain questions are invasions of privacy, whether the major scales measure what they purport to measure, what interpretations are valid from specific scales and scale clusters, etc. The MMPI, however, is an extensively used instrument and will likely continue to be so for some time to come.

III. FACTORS TO CONSIDER IN TESTING

A number of other considerations must be given to effective use, administration, organization and interpretation of tests. Some of these concepts are treated here. Others require more systematic investigation elsewhere.

A. Administering Tests

The person administering tests either to groups in a school situation or to an individual pupil must be thoroughly familiar with the administration guidelines in the test manual. Furthermore, the examiner must be aware of frequently neglected factors in the test situation itself. Such matters as *coaching* and *practice*, *giving socially desirable responses, guessing, faking, motivation*, the *physical conditions of testing* and the *qualities of the examiner* himself may alter the client's performance in unpredictable ways.

B. Test Interpretation

A test is a tool. It is useful and valuable only to the extent that it is administered properly, that it is appropriate to the persons taking the test and that accuracy and caution are observed in the interpretation and communication of the test data. Test interpretation is both a diagnostic and a counseling technique and deserves treatment from both points of view.

C. Criticisms of Testing

Particularly within the guidance movement, criticism of testing and the use of test data with school children has emerged. Some of these criticisms are worth noting.

1. *Tests may place labels on pupils which can have far-reaching effects on motivation and self-esteem.*

2. *By their empahsis on statistical average, tests may encourage narrow and conforming performance, reinforcing mediocrity.*

3. *Testing may too often emphasize mechanistic and impersonal ways of evaluating children.*

D. Organization of Testing Programs in Schools

The accumulation of data about individual pupils is a process which should be characterized by parsimony. Too much information, especially if it is not in use, only can lead to confusion and inefficiency. While there are numerous "minimal" testing programs, two organizational methods are presented in Table I.

TABLE 1
Minimal Testing Programs

Grade	Method 1	Method 2*
K	Reading Readiness	Intelligence
1	Intelligence	
2		Achievement
3	Intelligence	Intelligence
4	Diagnostic Reading	
5		Achievement
6	Achievement	
7		
8		Achievement
9	Interest/Intelligence/Achievement	
10		Intelligence
11	Interest	Achievement
12	Achievement	

*Aptitude, Personality and Interests Tests given on a need basis.

E. National Testing Programs

The boom in the testing movement has brought with it numerous national examination programs. A knowledge of these resources may aid the counselor or the guidance specialist responsible for the test programming in correctly planning the school testing program.

1. *College Entrance Examination Board.*
2. *Preliminary Scholastic Aptitude Tests.*
3. *American College Testing Program.*
4. *National Merit Scholarship Qualifying Test.*
5. *National Guidance Testing Program.*

F. Source of Information About Tests

Organizations providing the latest information about tests are numerous. The major sources are listed below.

1. *California Test Bureau,* Del Monte Research Park, Monterey, California, 93940.
2. *Educational Testing Service,* Princeton, New Jersey, 08540.
3. *The Psychological Cooperation,* 304 East 45th Street, New York, New York, 10017.
4. *Science Research Associates, Chicago,* 259 East Erie Street, Chicago, Illinois, 60611.
5. *The Sixth Mental Measurements Yearbook,* (Buros, O.K. Ed.,) Highland Park, New Jersey. Gryphon Press, 1965.

IV. STATISTICAL CONCEPTS RELATED TO APPRAISAL

Most psychological examiners, diagnosticians and school counselors must be acquainted with statistical concepts if they are to adequately function in the testing and appraisal service. A course in basic descriptive statistics is often essential for one to become involved with clinical appraisal devices. For some testing manuals, however, fewer statistical concepts are necessary to evaluate the test. Some of these *most* basic concepts are treated here.

A. Frequency Distribution

A frequency distribution is simply a way of presenting scores.

Typically, the frequency distribution is tabulation of scores running from low to high, and showing the number of persons who obtained each score. Scores are grouped together in broad categories.

B.   Normal Curve

The normal curve is defined as a curve which represents the frequency of occurrence of data for each value of a variable when these variations are said to arise from a large number of random causes. The normal curve is the familiar bell-shaped curve which can be used to derive quantities which make one pupil's test scores comparable with others.

C.   Measure of Central Tendency

Frequently we wish to know in a group of scores, the average or middle score. There are three basic types of measures of central position in such distributions of scores.

1. *Mean.*

The mean is the average score and is computed by summing all of the raw scores and dividing by the number of scores.

2. *Median.*

The most typical score, or the score in a distribution in which 50 percent of the cases fall on either side of it, is the median. The median is useful when distribution of scores is not normal and where the mean score would be misleading.

3. *Mode.*

The mode, a crude measure of central position, is the most frequently occuring score.

D.   Measures of Dispersion or Variation

Not only are the central tendencies of a distribution of interest, but often one wishes to know the degree of scatter or variance from the center. Measures of variance provide a measure of distance, therefore, from the center.

1. *Range.*

The most primitive measure of dispersion is the range, defined simply as the distance between the highest and lowest scores in a distribution.

2. *Interquartile Range.*

One half the distance between two quartile points is the measure of dispersion called the interquartile range. A *quartile* is one of three points that divide the number of cases in a distribution into four equal parts, the lowest quartile containing the bottom 25 percent of the scores, etc.

3. *Standard Deviation.*

The standard deviation is the most basic tool for interpreting test scores. The standard deviation is a measure of cluster around the mean in a normal curve. Sixty-eight percent of the scores will fall within one standard deviation on either side of the mean.

E.   Measures of Comparison

Generally measures of comparison are statistical means of comparing two or more sets of scores.

1. *Correlation.*

A coefficient of correlation is a mathmetical index of the degree to which two measures vary together. The index varies from −1.00, denoting an inverse or opposite relationship, to +1.00 denoting perfect correspondence. A coefficient of +.00 indicates no relationship between variables. The Pearson product-moment correlation is most widely used in testing.

2. *Tests of Significance.*

Sometimes tests are employed to see whether two or more differences in scores are the differences or whether they are brought about by chance fluctuations. These statistical tests are more frequently used in research than in testing.

a. *Chi Square Test.*
b. *Student's t Test.*
c. *Analysis of Variance.*

F. Other Test Relevant Terms

While a glossary of terms in testing and measurement would be a useful resource for the student of appraisal, some minimum core of test relevant terms are essential for most school personnel having the least contact with tests.

1. *Percentile.*

A point in distribution below which is found the percentage of cases called the percentile. The 25th percentile is the point below which 25 percent of all scores fall.

2. *Standard Score.*

Any score in which raw scores have been transformed into expressions making comparability or interpretation easier is called a standard score.

a. *Z Scores.* One statistical yardstick which provides a comparison of an individual's score with the mean is the Z score. It is the deviation of the pupil's raw score from the mean of his group in relation to the standard deviation of the scores.

b. *Stanine.* Short for *Standard Nine,* the stanine is a standard score for a nine point scale of standard scores. It has a mean of 5, a standard deviation of 2, and a range between 1 and 9.

3. *Decile.*

The decile divides the distribution of scores along a percentile basis, dividing it into ten equal parts. The first decile equals the tenth percentile; the ninth decile equals the ninetieth percentile.

4. *Standard Error of Measurement.*

The standard error is the estimate of the size of the error of measurement in a score. All scores are unreliable to a certain extent.

5. *Random Sample.*

A sample of a population in which every individual in the

population has an equal chance of being chosen. The random sample attempts to estimate some characteristic in the population as a whole.

6. *Item Analysis.*

A statistical study of test results to determine the difficulty value of each item in a test, how well it discriminates and how well it correlates with some external criterion is the procedure known as item analysis.

7. *Correction for Guessing.*

In true-false or multiple choice tests, devices are employed to discourage guessing. Substracting rights minus some proportions of wrong answers is one procedure for correction.

8. *Factor Analysis.*

Any technique for analyzing a set or table of intercorrelations to uncover the underlying factors in the original variables is called factor analysis.

9. *Halo Effect.*

The tendency, in rating an individual, to let one of his traits or characteristics excessively influence ratings on other traits.

CHAPTER 17

APPRAISAL II: NONTEST TECHNIQUES

INTRODUCTION. Tests, particularly standardized tests, are systematic ways of observing behavior. Because tests involve a certain amount of rigor in administration and interpretation, many educators have come to feel that other methods may be employed to get to know the child better than by tests alone. Certainly talking to a child may provide the teacher or counselor more valuable information and clues, if handled sensitively, than many formalized tests. Nontest techniques are used to make up in breadth and depth what tests are not able to provide.

I. OBSERVATIONS

Observations are basic to nontest techniques. Sometimes observations may be systematic and highly reliable methods of recording some discreet characteristics of pupil behavior, e.g. the frequency of nail biting. Often they are informal devices for recording behavior which are highly dependent upon the observer, his background, frame of reference and experience. Certain fundamental characteristics are noteworthy for a background on observations.

A. Observations supplement other information
B. Observations fill in gaps left by other methods
C. Observations sample real behavior in its natural setting
D. Observations do not record all behavior but are selective
E. Observations facilitate the growth of the observers

II. ANECDOTAL RECORDS

The anecdotal record is an effective way for obtaining teacher or counselor observations of specific pupil behavior. It is a record of some significant behavior or events in the pupil's life. Anecdotal records are designed to facilitate staff understanding, but many times they may be abused by not being systematic or written properly. Certain criteria for good anecdotes are essential to maintain (Peters & Farwell, 1967).

A. Short, informal form should predominate
B. Significant events should be recorded
C. Reporting should be unbiased
D. Many types of students should be observed and reported
E. Observers should write the anecdotes
F. The form should be partitioned to allow interpretations and suggestions
G. Time preparing anecdotes should not be requisite by staff policy
H. Single anecdotes by themselves are not useful

III. RATING SCALES

Teachers, administrators and counselors are often asked to rate pupils on certain characteristics or traits. Usually the person being rated is evaluated on some predetermined set of criteria, e.g. honesty, courtesy, leadership, etc. The advantage of a rating scale is that it can easily be constructed for a variety of purposes. The disadvantage, however, is that errors may easily be made in constructing the scale or in evaluating the characteristics which are rated (Schertzer & Stone, 1966).

A. Types of Rating Scales

1. *Numerical Scales.*

Numbers can be used to denote gradations in meaning along one characteristic. A series of such graded characteristics make up a numerical rating scale.

2. *Descriptive Scales.*

Rather than using numbers to specify the extent of a characteristic, this type of scale uses phrases which are to be checked in order of degree, extent or severity.

3. *Graphic Scales.*

In this type of scale a characteristic is named, and descriptive categories of degree of this trait are listed on a continuum The observer evaluates the trait with a check on the continuum.

4. *Paired Comparisons.*

On this scale the rater is forced to compare each pupil with every other pupil on some trait according to limited categories of degree.

B. Cautions in Constructing Rating Scales

Since rating scales are easily subject to error, caution should characterize their construction.

1. *Traits should be clearly defined.*
2. *The trait should be observable.*
3. *Gradations in meaning should be carefully defined.*

IV. PUPIL DATA QUESTIONNAIRES

It is difficult to find school systems not employing some form of pupil data questionnaire. The items on these forms provide information concerning the pupil's home, habits, plans, etc. Ideally, a great deal of information can be gained from the proper and timely administration of these personal data sheets.

A. Criteria for Use

In order to protect the school and cumulative record from saturation of information, as well as to insure reliability of the data, some criteria are useful to consider before administration.

1. *What is the purpose of the questionnaire?*
2. *When will the questionnaire be used?*
3. *Who will administer it?*
4. *Who will analyze the data?*

B. Advantages and Disadvantages

The pupil data questionnaire can potentially offer comprehensive information about the ongoing life of the student which may be missed on another appraisal device. The limitations, however, are whether, and how much personal information the school has a right to obtain, and how this data, once obtained, will be organized, analyzed, interpreted and communicated.

V. AUTOBIOGRAPHIES

The autobiography is a self-reporting device which serves as another tool for recording aspects of student behavior and also provides an element of freedom of expression and relevation of attitudes and emotions which might not be otherwise tapped in appraisal. These positive benefits, however, are only possible when the autobiography is handled in confidence and discretion.

A. Types of Autobiographies

1. *Structured.*

The structured autobiography usually follows some predetermined outlined covering past, present and future topics.

2. *Unstructured.*

The unstructured autobiography is an open-ended device which may allow greater freedom of expression for some, but may likely prove difficult to interpret.

B. Interpreting Autobiographies

Certain guidelines have been suggested for handling and interpreting the pupil autobiography.

1. *What is the general impression of the document: appearance, length, style and composition?*
2. *Are there any noticeable omissions, inaccuracies and incongruities?*
3. *Does the pupil employ defensive mechanisms or distinguish feelings from facts?*
4. *Is the document comprehensive?*

VI. DIARIES

The diary is a daily, or weekly, reporting by the pupil of significant events and feelings. It is useful as a pupil-focused instrument to the extent that some rapport and open atmosphere exists for the pupil to authentically document events in his life. The diary is sometimes called the *daily log*.

VII. SOCIOGRAM

The sociogram is a pictorial representation of specific relationships among group members. It is constructed from information given by the group itself.

A. Purpose of the Sociogram

In general sociometric methods are used to assess the adequacy of pupil interpersonal relations and acceptance by peers. Theoretically it is a measure of each individual's *social stimulus value* within a particular group.

B. Construction of the Sociogram

The sociogram can be used in a multitude of ways. Usually the teacher asks the children a question regarding who they would most like to sit next to in class. Second choices may also be taken. Procedures in sociometry exist for the tabulation of these patterns of choices and the construction of a graph illustrating those pupils chosen most often, those chosen least, etc.

C. Basic Sociometric Terms

While sociometry has expanded into a distinct technique used in many quarters, its terminology has grown with it. Some of the more fundamental terms are worth noting.

1. *Star.*

A Star is an individual receiving a relatively large portion of choices in the group.

2. *Isolate.*

A group member receiving no choices from other group members is called an isolate.

3. *Neglectee.*

A neglectee is one receiving proportionately few choices by the group.

4. *Rejectee.*

When the sociometric device is so structured as to provide negative choices (e.g. who would you least like to sit next to?) the individual receiving a large proportion of these negative choices is a rejectee.

5. *Sociometric Clique.*

When a subgroup of the class choose each other with a few outside choices, this patterning is referred to as sociometric clique.

VIII.   CASE STUDIES

The case history is a cumulative itemization of data about a child covering some span of time. It can be one of the most comprehensive techniques for appraising an individual in the entire arsenal of devices used in the appraisal service. The case study helps to clarify, organize and summarize information needed for understanding aspects of pupil behavior.

A.   Levels of the Case Study

The case study technique can be used for different purposes corresponding to different levels of analysis.

1. *Teacher-pupil analysis and review.*
2. *Teacher-counselor review and appraisal.*
3. *Guidance-team analysis including case conference handling and referrals.*
4. *Institutional-administrative evaluation and appraisal.*

B.   Constituents of the Case Study

Few school programs are so well staffed that each pupil becomes the focus of the case study. Doubtless value would be achieved if such were the case, since not all pupils have problems needing such systematic and specialized attention. In order to keep the case study a viable and effective device, certain recommendations regarding its make-up are worth observing.

1. *Identifying Features.*

Personal data about the child is included here: age, class, etc.

2. *Family History.*

Here socio-economic status, movements, notable events (divorces, separations) are of interest.

3. *Childhood Events.*

Notation here is made of significant events in the life of the pupil during preschool years.

4. *Educational History.*

The educational history provides not only information on schools attended, but learning successes and failures, friends and special instruction.

5. *Health History.*

The health history gives an overview of childhood diseases, pre and post-natal birth effects, immunizations and any special medical services.

6. *Social History.*

The social history marks any important episodes in the child's life including current evaluations.

7. *Test Profiles.*

Concise summaries of diagnostic evaluations make up this central feature of the case study.

8. *Work History.*

Depending on the age of the pupil, a summary of the length and type of work experiences and notable successes and failures are included.

9. *Personal Interests.*

Some mention should be made in the case study of special interest, hobbies and aspirations of the child.

10. *Referrals.*

Any previous treatment given by referral, as well as the reasons for referral, should be noted.

IX. CUMULATIVE RECORDS

Most schools use a record keeping system which stores vital information on each child. Since the cumulative record is used by administrators, teachers and guidance staff, it frequently fails to provide the comprehensive picture of the pupil for which it is intended. Nonetheless, this composite of data from school personnel on the child can serve as a dynamic resource if the data to be included is selected and recorded conscientiously.

A. Information Included in the Cumulative Record

1. *Personal and Family Data.*
2. *Medical Information.*
3. *Schools attended, Entry Dates, Transcripts.*
4. *Test Results.*
5. *School Activities.*
6. *Anecdotal Records, Autobiographies and Trait Ratings.*

B. Problems in the Use of Cumulative Records

Without frequent review and evaluation, the cumulative record may get to contain, over time, information potentially harmful to the family or child if used in the wrong way. Attention should be given to what entries are made in the record, how often the record is reviewed, and what personnel have access to them.

CHAPTER 18

VOCATIONAL AND CAREER DEVELOPMENT THEORY

INTRODUCTION. The history of vocational development, treated in previous chapters, marks an important event with the establishment of the Vocational Bureau in Boston in 1908 by Frank Parsons. The approach to choosing a vocation was considered a one-step event of matching the characteristics of an individual with the requirements of the job. Vocational guidance has come a long way since the days of Parsons, and it is currently felt that making any occupational choice, developing a career pattern or selecting an appropriate educational goal is not a single discrete event, but a continuous process of development which is grounded in the elementary school or perhaps earlier. Vocational counseling, therefore, is not just placement or finding the right job for the right student, but it encompasses a wide range of past, present and future factors which must be studied and understood for the student to achieve his vocational maturity.

I. FACTORS INFLUENCING CAREER DEVELOPMENT

A great number of variables can be seen to affect the career pattern. The crippled child is automatically barred from certain occupational possibilities later in life. Racial factors may inhibit entry into certain occupational or educational roles. The psychological factors alone are numerous for understanding the vocational development process.

A. Intelligence

Some occupations require different levels of intelligence than others. The intelligence quotients of laborers versus doctors is

194

striking in its disparity. On the other hand, counselors can easily make the mistake of treating the low-intelligence child as if he were automatically unqualified for occupational roles to which he aspires. Intelligence quotients cannot be the sole indicators of whether one child's *level of aspiration* is realistic or not. Other factors such as motivation, personality and aptitude must also be considered.

B. Aptitude

Aptitudes are more or less related to certain types of occupations. A high mathematical aptitude may be characteristic of professional accountants. Aptitudes predict future achievement and should a particular meaningful pattern of aptitudes emerge in a testing situation, the client in counseling may begin selecting certain occupational groups over others on the basis of predicted future performance.

C. Personality Characteristics

The characteristics of extraversion, aggressiveness and independence may be well suited to the population of car salesmen, but may be fatal for entry into monastic life. Personality characteristics are more relevant to some occupations than others. Again, however, caution should be used in interpreting personality test data to vocational aspirants since no clear cut relationships have been established between occupational groups and personality, and most personality tests are unreliable to some extent.

D. Interests

Another device which has been used to assess an individual's compatibility with an occupational type is his interest pattern. Theoretically, an individual with similar interests to those persons employed in some occupation, would feel and do better in that occupation than a person without those interests. The variability in interest profiles, however, as well as the overlapping nature of interests with different occupations make specific predictions and assessments from interest patterns a difficult task.

E. Environmental Factors

The environment is a general rubric for numbers of variables which can affect occupational choice. The socio-economic status of an individual, for example, may have great impact on the values placed on education in the home, the ability to pay for training in specialized occupations, and the levels of aspiration for particular positions. Access and entry into occupations are frequently governed by factors other than psychological ones, e.g. racial, religious or sexual discrimination. These environmental determinants must be addressed in any theory of vocational development.

II. THEORIES OF VOCATIONAL DEVELOPMENT

A theory provides a systematic way of looking at phenomena. It is a model to organize and predict facets of the occupational picture and the individual as he interfaces with it.

A. General Theoretical Models

Because there are so many theories of vocational development, it has been suggested that some of these approaches should be classified in terms of the general orientations which they take. Most of these models are not entirely homogeneous and overlap each other to a great extent.

1. *Trait-factor Model.*

This, the oldest approach to occupational choice, is a model deriving from the Parsonian approach and assumes that there should be a straightforward matching of an individual's abilities, intelligence, aptitudes and interests with the specific characteristics of the occupation.

2. *Sociological Model.*

Certain external situations exist, independent of the efforts of an individual, which condition and determine the gross occupational groupings which he will enter. In this model, social determinants predominate in conditioning occupational choice.

3. *Developmental Model.*

The developmental theories stress that an individual at different stages of growth develops occupational images and stereotypes which he selects to try out and test until one makes a suitable fit with his self-concept and view of reality.

4. *Personality Model.*

People select occupations in order to satisfy their personal needs. It is these constellations of needs which determine the selection of an occupation, the satisfaction given by the occupation and the stability of the occupational choice.

B. Eli Ginzberg's Theory of Occupational Choice

Ginzberg and his associates have assumed three basic elements in a theory of occupational choice (1951).

1. *Process.*

Occupational choice is a process which follows a developmental pattern. As such, it has been analyzed by Ginzberg in terms of a succession of stages.

a. *Fantasy period.* Covering the eleven to seventeen age period, the period of tentative choices is characterized by four basic substages.

(1) Interest stage. The child develops patterns of likes and dislikes in terms of a career direction.
(2) Capacity stage. At this period of time the adolescent begins to think about his career directions in terms of his own abilities and capacities rather than simply on a like-dislike basis.
(3) Value stage. Here the individual begins to evaluate the *meaningfulness* of different choices and life styles.
(4) Transition stage. Nearing the close of the high school years, the individual begins to face the realtiy of making concrete vocational decisions.

c. *Realistic period.* The realistic period is thought to come into prominence between the ages of eighteen and twenty-two.

(1) Exploratory stage. While there is still flexibility of planning, this period is marked by a narrowing of goals and exploration of limited career objectives.

(2) Crystallization stage. At this time the individual makes definite decisions and commitments.

(3) Specification stage. Narrower alternatives are examined and specialization occurs.

2. *Irreversibility.*

Ginzberg contends that the process of choice development is largely irreversible.

3. *Compromise.*

The final element of the general theory is that each choice the individual makes is a compromise between his interests and desires, on the one hand, and his capacities on the other.

C. Anne Roe's Need Theory of Vocational Choice

Roe's theory holds that each person's genetic background and the early patterning of need satisfactions and frustrations in combination with the types and manners of childhood experiences determine the basic interest pattern of the adult, and this constellation determines the individual's vocational choice (1957).

1. *Need Hierarchy.*

Some needs are more basic than others and can thus be organized into a hierarchy. The *intensity* of the needs, the *frequency* of their satisfaction, their *delay* in satisfaction all determine which needs are unconscious and dominant motivators. Scaling the need hierarchy depends on how well earlier, more basic needs, have been satisfied. The hierarchy is taken from *Maslow's* system.

a. *Physiological needs.*
b. *The need for safety.*
c. *The need for love.*
d. *The need for independence and self-esteem.*
e. *The need for information.*
f. *The need for understanding.*
g. *The need for beauty.*
h. *The need for self-actualization.*

2. *Childhood Experiences.*

An important factor in which needs become most dominant for the child is determined by the experiences which he has, and these are most likened to the manner in which his parents treated him. These parental orientations can be classified and in turn, lead to major orientations of the child.

a. *Concentration of emotion on the child.* An overprotecting or overdemanding attitude on the child is a form of this parental orientation.

b. *Avoidance of the child.* A second orientation which conditions the major need orientation of the child is an avoidant one in which the child is either neglected or in some way rejected.

c. *Acceptance of the child.* There are two forms of acceptance which Roe describes, a casual acceptance or a loving acceptance.

3. *Occupational Classification.*

The parental orientations, in combination with genetic inheritance and the need structure, result in the child's major orientations, e.g. *toward persons* (self or others) and *away from persons.* These orientations are correlated to major occupational groupings.

a. *Service.*
b. *Business.*
c. *Organizational.*
d. *Technological.*
e. *Recreational.*
f. *Scientific.*
g. *Cultural.*
h. *Artistic.*

D. Donald Super's Self-Concept Theory of Vocational Development.

Super's approach to vocational development is that he sees the process as a continuous development whereby the individual attempts to implement his self-concept in an occupation. The theory itself is complex, but its basic principles are worthy of review (1953).

1. *Individual Differences.*

By virtue of the fact that each individual possesses a unique set of capacities, interests and personality characteristics, he is thereby qualified for a number of occupations which find such types of characteristics suitable.

2. *Flexibility.*

The personal requirements of an occupation are not absolute, but allow some tolerance of differential psychological traits. As such, there are many occupations for each individual and many individuals for each occupation.

3. *Continuity and Synthesis.*

The environment in which people develop is continually in flux. The self-concepts of individuals, therefore, are equally in the process of change and development. One's choice and adjustment to an occupation is thus a continuous flow of synthesizing elements, not a single or irreversible event.

4. *Phases of Development.*

This continuous developmental process may be examined at certain stages in which self-concepts are formed, translated and finally implemented into the occupational picture.

  a. *Growth.*
  b. *Exploratory stage.*

  (1) Fantasy period.
  (2) Tentative period.
  (3) Realistic period.

  c. *Establishment stage.*

  (1) Trial.
  (2) Stable.

  d. *Maintenance stage.*
  e. *Decline.*

5. *Career Patterns.*

The occupational level which the individual attains and the

frequency and length of stable jobs is determined by the person's personality, his intelligence and socio-economic level.

6. *Developmental Process.*

The process of moving through the life stages is basically one of compromise between the self-concept and reality. The patterning is determined by the interactions between genetic and physiological make up, childhood and school experiences, opportunities to role play occupational styles, either in counseling or in real life, and the provisions for other exploratory experiences.

7. *Satisfaction.*

The degree to which work and life satisfaction is found is dependent upon the degree to which the self-concept is translated and implemented.

E. John Holland's Personality Topology

Holland's theory of vocational choice attempts to correlate certain personality types with certain psychological environments in order to empirically predict what vocational choices an individual will make (1959).

1. *Basic Assumptions.*

    a. *Vocational choices express personality.*
    b. *Interest inventories measure personality characteristics.*
    c. *Members of a vocation have similar personalities.*
    d. *Such similarities in personality lead to the construction of vocationally characteristic interpersonal environments.*
    e. *A person's satisfaction, achievement and stability in a vocation is determined by the congruence between his personality and the psychological environment in which he works.*
    f. *Our knowledge of vocational life must be more integrated with general psychological knowledge.*

2. *Personality Types.*

The personality type of an individual is assessed by the *Voca-*

tional Preference Inventory in which a person's pattern of interests is related to a major and minor personality type. The basic personality types are derived from interest patterns.

a. *Realistic.* The realistic type asserts himself through athletic and motor skills.

b. *Intellectual.* The intellectual type is characterized by self-control and insularity.

c. *Social.* Two characteristics of the social type are a need for close personal relations and dependency.

d. *Conventional.* The conventional personality seeks tasks which involve systematic and routine procedures.

e. *Enterprising.* The entreprenurial type is characterized by extroversion, verbal facility and aggressiveness.

f. *Artistic.* The artistic type is distinguished by a rejection of convention.

3. *Environmental Types.*

Environmental types are assessed by Holland's *Environmental Assessment Techniques.* The types are determined by the tasks which they require and are classified, similarly with personalities, into *realistic, intellectual, social, conventional, enterprising* and *artistic* environments. A realistic environment, for example, emphasizes concrete skills and motor tasks.

4. *Interactions.*

There are many ways in which personality types may interact with environments. The *congruence, consistency* and *homogeneity* of the interactions predict vocational choices, stability, achievement and satisfaction. An artistic personality in a conventional environment, for example, would exemplify an *incongruent* interaction.

F.   David Tiedeman and Robert O'Hara's Vocational Development Model

Vocational or career development is considered a process of carving out a vocational identity. In facing the problem of work, the personality engages in two processes: *differentation* and *integration.* These processes are the mechanisms of vocational development. Differentiation is the separation of some part or aspect of the vocational choice situation from the larger whole. Integration is the putting together of these differentiated parts into a new context. A model for this choice process is given.

1. *Anticipation.*

The beginning of the decision process is concerned with expecting and becoming preoccupied with the alternatives.
   a. *Exploration of alternatives and goals.*
   b. *Crystallization of alternatives.*
   c. *Choice.*
   d. *Clarification and elaboration of the decision*

2. *Implementation.*

Putting a decision into action and adjusting to its implications and consequences is a second major part of decision-making.
   a. *Induction into the experience.*
   b. *Reformation or an assertive immersion into the field as a consequence of acceptance and success.*
   c. *Integration and synthesis of individual beliefs with the external attitudes of others.*

COMMENTARY: None of the six theories treated here represents an entirely comprehensive model which explains why individuals choose one occupation over another and how they progress through that vocational choice. Instead, each theory emphasizes different points of focus. Roe's emphasis takes the vocational decision back into genetic history and early childhood experiences which shape the child's make-up of needs. Super and Ginzberg emphasize that the child's needs and personality characteristics progressively find their way into his developing self-concept, his identifications and self-images, and these are increasingly translated from his inner world (fantasy periods) into various stages of reality contact until occupational crystallization and specification occur. Holland sees the relationship between translating one's inner self-concept into an occupational self-concept best expressed as a kind of translation of one's personality types and subtypes into the various psycho-occupational types and subtypes of environments. Whether the person is compatible and satisfied with his choice of occupation is determined by the kind of interaction his personality makes with his psychological environment. The contribution of Tiedeman, and O'Hara on the other hand appears to fall less in the area of a developmental position which, like Super's and Ginzberg's suggests the individual progresses through certain stages of development and vocational maturity. Rather, their telelogical hypothesis suggests an individual making any vocational decision goes through a series of stages of decision-making itself. If this process is known, and an ideal decision-making model developed, then it is possible to use the choice model in a role-playing situation or as a simulation activity, to rehearse or develop greater decision-making effectiveness in clients, regardless of their developmental "level." Furthermore, computerization of this process becomes increasingly likely.

The theories treated here, while they have a certain commonality, nonetheless are nested in controversy. Such issues as the irreversibility of occupational choices, the relative importance of childhood needs, the potency of personality and interest variables versus social and environmental variables, and the timing of various stages of occupational development for various groups and subgroups are just some issues which are contested.

CHAPTER **19**

COUNSELING AND GUIDANCE
IN THE ELEMENTARY SCHOOL

INTRODUCTION. The development of guidance programs in elementary schools is relatively new. In many respects, elementary counseling guidance has unique characteristics which differ considerably from guidance at other levels of implementation. For this reason it is treated in a separate chapter.

I. REASONS FOR THE DEVELOPMENT
OF ELEMENTARY GUIDANCE

In recent years guidance has wrenched itself from a purely vocational activity to a function and a service which encompasses far more than mere occupational and educational planning and placement. Elementary guidance is one example of this development. A number of factors are responsible for this change in focus.

A. Influence of Child Development

The vast amounts of work in child psychology and child development have pointed up the importance of the elementary years in shaping future behavior patterns.

B. Educating the Whole Child

Increased emphasis upon the education of the whole child has come as a result of the progressive education movement. The logical corollary of this trend is a downward extension of guidance services in the schools.

C. Early-Decision-making

As our society has become more complex, the choices and decisions which must be made in determining a life style have become telescoped, requiring earlier and earlier choices and tentative choices.

D. Prevention

The problems of school drop-outs, juvenile delinquency, under-achievement, antisocial attitudes can only be worked with at a symptomatic level in the secondary school. In order to focus upon the root causes of these social ailments from a preventive point of view, the forerunners of these problems must be recognized early, in the elementary school, and dealt with at that time.

II. APPROACHES TO ELEMENTARY GUIDANCE

Just as there are model approaches and orientations to guidance in the secondary school, so too are there approach models for elementary guidance programming (Cottingham, 1965).

A. Service Approach

The service approach to elementary guidance is most akin to secondary school programs in its emphasis upon the provision of some of the same basic services, e.g. appraisal service, information service and counseling service.

B. Teaching Approach

There are many who see guidance as an activity performed by the classroom teacher rather than a specialist. In this model of elementary guidance the teacher takes guidance as a means toward effective teaching.

C. Specialist Approach

The specialist model sees the elementary guidance function as implemented through a team effort of school social workers, counselors, physicians, psychometrists, etc.

D. Child Study Approach

Similar to the specialist approach, the child study model implements guidance only to certain students needing in-depth study by a team of specialists who can provide the attention and resources needed by special students.

E. Coordinated Approach

The coordinated plan for elementary guidance is one which emphasizes a fusion of efforts between the teacher, the principal and those guidance specialists who may be part of the guidance program.

F. Development Approach

Developmental guidance is a model which applies to all levels of school implementation, but is particularly relevant to the elementary level. It approaches the child in terms of his knowing, understanding and accepting of himself, emphasizing the child's strengths, his individuality and his goal-oriented choice making behavior through the process of maturation and growth.

III. PROBLEMS OF ELEMENTARY SCHOOL CHILDREN

Most problems of the elementary school child are prototypic of problems later seen in the junior school or secondary school. No classification scheme exists, however, which provides some taxonomy of counseling-related problems. Some overall system is proposed.

A. Psycho-motor Difficulties

Children with problems in *handedness, laterality, balance* and coordination may express these seemingly discrete developmental problems in lowered academic achievement and poor self-concept development. As such, psycho-motor difficulties perceptual-motor and sensori-motor difficulties have relevance to the guidance function.

B. Psychobiologic Difficulties

Children often express their emotional difficulties in somatic ways. Similarly, somatic complaints may result in disturbances in psychological and academic functioning. Children with nausea, headaches, dizziness, nonspecific pains, low grade fevers, nervousness, etc., may not only be seen by the school nurse but may come under the attention of the counselor.

C. Psycho-social Difficulties

Interpersonal difficulties include teasing, fighting, rivalry, delinquency and acting-out, as well as withdrawal, isolation, insecurity, daydreaming, etc. These problems are often noticed by the teacher and may have roots in a home situation. When they are chronic, however, they may become enough to warrant a referral to the counselor.

D. Psycho-educational Difficulties

Under this rubric, fall all of those academic difficulties which affect a child's emotional well-being. As a child progresses through each grade level, he is exposed to success and failure (in sometimes unpredictable amounts), and these reinforcements contribute to his interpersonal adjustment, his self-concept and his general school adjustment. Problems of children, which appear the result of school failure, may be less focused in the child himself and more related to his exposure to bad teaching and/or an inappropriate curriculum. On the other hand, the child may have a pattern of specific academic or psycholinguistic deficits which predispose him to failure. The role of the counselor, as a consultant to the teacher in helping her appraise individual student's deficits and in facilitating her development of an individualized and meaningful curriculum for particular children, is further supported with this class of difficulties.

IV. THEORETICAL APPROACHES
WITH SPECIAL APPLICABILITY

Most counseling approaches discussed in the chapter on Systems and Theories of counseling can be implemented, with modifications, in the elementary school. Differences between client centered counseling, both individual and group, are largely quantitative as this approach goes from the secondary to the elementary level. Other theoretical models also have similar applicability. Two approaches, however, have special relevance.

A. Play Therapy

Adults may be asked to "free associate" or let anything which occurs to them come into consciousness. Children do not respond to free association as a therapeutic technique. Originating in psychoanalysis, therefore, the use of play as a means of expressing fantasy and emotional tension in therapy was developed. Currently play is used by many practitioners as a release mechanism for children. Its applications in diagnosis, in developing rapport in counseling, and in teaching are numerous.

B. Behavioral Counseling

The use of operant principles in counseling and in the classroom is receiving increasing attention. Counseling is conceived as a process of learning and relearning. The learning process occurs both in the counseling interview and outside it. The counselor is frequently a consultant to the teacher in helping her treat specific children and in maintaining an effective learning environment. The teacher, by the systematic application of reinforcement principles, facilitates specific behavior change. She rewards behavior which approximates specific goals and she does not reinforce (ignores) maladaptive behavior patterns on the assumption that they will extinguish. John D. Krumboltz is most associated with the behavioral model in counseling.

V. DIFFERENCES BETWEEN ELEMENTARY AND SECONDARY GUIDANCE

To some extent guidance in the elementary school focuses more upon development of the child in his total context and in his personal-social adjustment than secondary guidance. A number of specific factors differentiate elementary and secondary guidance however, apart from this general difference in approach.

A. Personnel Involved

Typically, the elementary guidance program relies more heavily upon the teacher for implementation while secondary guidance tends toward the use of specialists to a greater extent.

B. Services Offered

More emphasis is placed in the secondary school upon occupation and educational planning than at the elementary level.

C. Counselor Duties

At the elementary level the role of the counselor as a consultant to teachers is more pronounced than in the secondary school where the counselor usually spends most of his time working directly with students. Such a distinction, however, is rapidly losing its clarity as elementary counselors increasingly are directly involved in counseling with individual and groups of children.

D. Problems

Secondary school pupils have problems chiefly concerning learning success, heterosexual relationships, health and career planning. Elementary school children tend to differ significantly from these concerns.

E. Counselor-student Ratios

The currently recommended ratios of counselors to pupils in the elementary school is 1: 600, while in the secondary school only 1: 250. The rationale for this differential is, however, questionable.

F. Costs

The estimated cost per pupil in the elementary school is $20.00 and at the secondary level $30.00. This, too, is changing very rapidly.

VI. ROLES OF THE ELEMENTARY SCHOOL COUNSELOR

Counselor training programs are increasingly offering specialization in elementary school counseling. This fact signifies the variation in role between elementary and secondary counselors. The chief duties of the elementary counselor are listed.

A. Consultation With Teachers

As already mentioned, a greater emphasis is placed upon teacher-counselor contracts at the elementary level. The counselor may assist the teacher in implementing some recommendations in the classroom. The counselor may also consult with the teacher on curriculum and general instructional content.

B. Counseling With Children

The counselor conducts individual and group counseling with children either referred by the teacher, administration or parents, or with self-referred children.

C. Resource and Referral Agent

The counselor is a resource for the school in helping teachers become more fully acquainted with a guidance orientation and with the developmental characteristics of their pupils. The counselor also acts as a resource for parents in assisting them with their needs and problems in dealing with their youngster. Moreover, the counselor is a referral agent for health, social and psychological services which the community or school may offer for the special child.

D. Appraisal

The counselor uses appraisal information to assist the child toward greater self-understanding and awareness, and also to facilitate teacher understanding of the child's special needs.

VII. AREAS OF CONTROVERSY IN ELEMENTARY GUIDANCE

The newness of elementary guidance brings with it some divergence and disagreement about certain fundamental questions concerning its growth. The rationale for each position is too lengthy to document, but a general awareness of the points of controversy is worthwhile.

A. Should all elementary guidance service be developmental?

B. What kind of a balance should there be between direct services to children and consultant services with teachers and parents?

C. Should the teacher be the sole guidance agent or should the team concept be stressed in providing specific services.

D. To what degree should the counselor become involved with vocational development?

PART IV

SPECIAL TOPICS

CHAPTER 20

MENTAL RETARDATION, LEARNING DISABILITIES AND UNDERACHIEVEMENT

INTRODUCTION. While it may appear that underachievement, certain forms of learning disability and mental retardation belong more properly in the area of special education than counseling psychology and guidance, these problems and syndromes may come to the attention of the counselor in remote or indirect ways and are for these reasons worthy of some treatment as special topics.

I. MENTAL RETARDATION

Mental retardation refers to a certain degree of below average intellectual functioning arising during the developmental period of an individual, which is associated with impairment in maturation, learning and/or social adjustment. Previously, mentally retarded persons were classified as idiots, imbeciles and morons. These terms have been disregarded and substituted with other means of classifying intellectual functioning. Usually mental deficiency is categorized on an IQ basis, at least in part; four levels of mental deficiency are usually described; profound, severe, moderate and mild.

A. Severe and Profound Retardation

These persons typically have IQs estimated to be below 35. They function at an intellectual level less than that of a 3 year old child and are unable to master even the simplest tasks; most are institutionalized or dependent all of their lives. Certain syndromes are common to this group.

1. *Mongolism.*

The mongoloid is typified with thick skin of the eyelids, a deep transverse fissure in the tongue, closeset, deep eyes, thick stubby hands, deformities of the ears and almond-shaped eyes. Some 10 percent of all hospitalized mental defectives are mongoloid. Mongolism appears to find its etiology in a chromosomal aberration.

2. *Cretinism.*

Symptoms of cretinism include dwarfism, short thick legs, a large head, height of somewhat over three feet, a short thick neck, delayed sexual development, dry, scaly skin and general sluggishness. Incidence of cretinism is about 5 percent of institutionalized mental defectives. Etiology appears related to thyroid failure and a lack of iodine. Early treatment may bring about a restoration of normal intelligence.

3. *Microcephaly.*

Another description of microcephaly is "small headedness." The head is of a conical shape, with inadequate growth of the brain. The forehead recedes as well as the chin. It is a rare syndrome with a mixed etiology. No treatment is known.

4. *Hydrocephaly.*

Symptoms of hydrocephaly include slightness of the body, large headedness, degeneration of the optic nerves and occasional convulsions. Fluid within the cranium causes damage to the brain tissue and is responsible for the enlarged head. Surgery may be effective.

5. *Other forms.*

Other syndromes have been differentiated by constitute rare forms of profound and severe retardation. These include *Tay-Sachs disease, Turner's syndrome, gargoylism, Phenylketonuria, Dwarfism and Macrocephaly* (Hutt and Gibby, 1965; Coleman, 1964).

B. Moderate Retardation

Individuals manifesting moderate mental deficiency possess

an IQ of between 35 and 50. These persons have a slow learning rate, are physically slow and may suffer from certain deformities. They function at an intellectual level of a child from 4 to 7 years of age, and some may be taught to read, write and become partially independent in adulthood.

C. Mild Retardation

This is the largest single category of mental deficiency, including more than 5 million persons. Mild retardation covers an IQ range of from 50 to 70, approximating an intellectual level of a child 8 to 11 years of age. These individuals may achieve a larger degree of independence and may be trained for a variety of occupations. Sociocultural and socioeconomic factors appear to contribute to a greater degree than genetic or biochemical factors in the etiology of this type of retarded intellectual capacity.

The most frequent form of mild deficiency is called *cultural-familial retardation;* no evidence of brain pathology is involved, but it has a tendency to run in families. Most of these retardates come from families at the lower end of the economic spectrum and some mixture of cultural, economic and perhaps, genetic factors may give rise to the syndrome.

II. DISTRIBUTION AND CLASSIFICATION OF INTELLIGENCE

Intelligence classifications have been developed with well standardized individual intelligence tests. The following classificatory scheme is given to provide the student with an overview of the distribution of intelligence in the United States. It is based upon the Wechsler Adult Intelligence Scale (Wechsler, 1955, p. 20).

A. Mental Defective

IQ range from 69 and below and includes 2.2 percent of the population.

B. Borderline

IQ ranges from 70 to 79 and 6.7 percent of the population is included in this area.

C. Dull Normal

IQ ranges from 80 to 89 with 16.1 percent of the population included.

D. Average

Average IQ varies from 90 to 109 on the WAIS and includes 50 percent of the population.

E. Bright Normal

IQ ranges from 110 to 119 and 16.1 percent of the population belongs to this group.

F. Superior

IQ ranges from 120 to 129; it represents 6.7 percent of the population.

G. Very Superior

IQ extends from 130 and above and 2.2 percent of the population belong to this category.

III. LEARNING DISABILITIES AND UNDERACHIEVEMENT

Two key concepts are important in the discussion of the underachieving and learning disabled child: *performance* and *potential*. The child who is mentally deficient has a low intellectual capacity or potential. His performance in school is likely to be severely impaired; in a way it is predicted that he perform at a lower level than other children his age. Underachievement, on the other hand, is shown by a child whose potential exceeds his performance. He falls below what might be predicted on the basis of his intelligence.

A. Definition of Learning Disabilities

The learning disabled child shows a deficit in learning even though he is of normal intelligence and neither emotionally disturbed nor physically handicapped.

B. Terminology

Learning disabilities represent a general label applied to children who have specific forms of underachievement or educational handicaps. Many theories have been forwarded to indicate that perceptual, cerebral, neurological or psychological factors may contribute to the learning deficit. As a result, many terms for learning disability have been generated.

1. *Minimal neurological dysfunction.*
2. *Psychoneurological learning disability.*
3. *Dyslexia.*
4. *Perceptually handicapped.*
5. *Hyperkinesis.*

C. Types of Learning Deficits

Learning disorders may be subdivided into two groups, those dealing with pre-skills in academic areas, and those dealing directly with academic functions themselves.

1. *Pre-skill deficits.*

A pre-skill deficit predisposes the child to failure in regular school subjects. Eye-hand coordination is a pre-skill to writing, just as is it to aiming a gun or playing basketball. Poor eye-hand coordination, therefore, may result in a writing disorder. Some pre-skill deficits are treated.

a. *Visual perceptual deficits.* These problems concern how a child deals with, interprets and uses visual stimuli. Figure-ground perception, visual discrimination and form constancy are examples of visual perceptual skills.

b. *Auditory perceptual deficits.* These difficulties concern how a child meaningfully interacts with auditory stimuli, i.e. how well he can discriminate sounds, how well he can pick up a signal disguised in a noisy background (figure-ground perception), etc.

c. *Gross motor deficits.* Motor abilities, such as balance and posture, laterality and directionality affect the child's acquisition of other skills, his concepts of spatial relations and his relationship to his body. Children with motor difficulties may also show a high incidence of reading handicap. Learning disabled children who are hyperactive (hyperkinesis) may have motor difficulties which interfere with attention and concentration.

2. *Academic deficits.*

Particular patterns of difficulty arise in each of the major subject matter areas in the elementary school. These include reading failure (dyslexia), arithmetic, spelling and writing disorders.

D. Treatment of Learning Disability: Diagnosis and Remediation

Typically, the classroom teacher refers the underachieving child for psychological diagnosis which determines the child's intellectual potential and his patterns of deficits and strengths. It also rules out the primacy of emotionality as the cause of the learning problem. At this point the diagnosis specifies certain skill areas to address. A prescription is usually written which makes curricular recommendations to the teacher and which asks her to tailor a curriculum to this child at his instructional levels, minimizing frustration and overstimulation, so that he can compensate for his learning deficit at his own pace and under conditions of positive reinforcement. This pattern of diagnosis and remediation is often called *prescriptive* or *individualized instruction* and requires open communication and cooperation between pupil personnel staff and instructional staff. Appropriate implementation of a psycho-educational prescription usually results in some improvement in the child's level of performance and his attitude toward the learning experience.

E. Role of the Counselor

The counselor is not likely to become as involved with mentally retarded children as he is with learning disabed students. He is, usually, only ancillary to the entire effort towards the child; a more central figure is the school psychologist, who participates directly in the diagnosis, and the teacher, who implements the prescription. The counselor, however, may be called upon to help facilitate the child's relationship with himself and the learning experience while the academic therapy is being implemented concurrently. Often learning disabled children have low and distorted self-concepts, strong feelings of inferiority, insecurity and alienation as well as a general nervousness over high expectations being placed upon them at home or in school. A palliative, supportive counseling relationship may be a meaningful activity to parallel the academic changes in the child's life. With hyperkinetic children who tend to act out and present discipline problems, a more structured but equally palliative approach is facilitative (Kroth, 1971).

CHAPTER **21**

THE PROBLEM OF DRUG ABUSE

INTRODUCTION. Within the last few years a new problem has engulfed the educational scene with untold ramifications for counselors, the school and society at large: drug abuse. The problem does not appear to be confined to a particular type of school, type of child or type of environment nor does it confine itself to colleges or secondary schools. Drug problems have been documented in elementary schools through graduate programs, and while there are differences in the incidence of drug abuse and in the kinds of drugs used at these different levels, one general conclusion is clear: drug abuse has and continues to grow at an extremely rapid rate in our society. Research on the nature of the drugs which are used, their characteristics and functions, as well as the incidence of drug abuse and those kinds of students who are predisposed toward the problem, is severely lacking. Some studies have reported upwards of 50 percent of secondary school students in a wealthy surburban school system as having experience with marihuana. Some large state universities report confidential polls showing 70 percent of the student body having tried marihuana and other drugs, with estimates of between 35 to 40 percent admitting regular use of these drugs. There are no clear answers to the problem, and the purpose of this chapter is to provide a familiarity with the kinds of problems and issues which drug abuse raises for our schools.

I. TYPES OF DRUGS

Drugs go by varying rubrics and slang, e.g. grass, pot, speed, acid, etc. Drug abuse has led, in many respects, to a drug culture having its own terminology, literature, music and politics. Marihuana is perhaps the most widely used drug, followed in frequency by the hallucinogens and the amphetamines. Below is a list of the major kinds of drugs and their specific characteristics. Not all of these drugs are used with equal frequency, and it is, for example, much less likely that cocaine is used with anything like the frequency of LSD or marihuana.

A. Marihuana

Marihuana is a mild hallucinogen which is most frequently taken by smoking, although it is sometimes taken orally. The drug itself is not physically addictive, but is classified under federal law as a narcotic.

B. Other Hallucinogens

While marihuana is thought of as a mild hallucinogen, its potency in this respect is markedly smaller than LSD. LSD is usually taken orally but may be taken by injection and reportedly, results in hallucinations, sharp distortions in time and space, increased sensitivity and awareness and may, with particular pre-morbid personalities or high dosages, result in psychotic episodes. LSD was brought under federal drug abuse control in 1966. Other hallucinogens which are in increasing use in schools are listed.

(1) *Mescaline.*
(2) *Psilocybin.*
(3) *Peyote.*
(4) *DMT.*

C. Amphetamines

Amphetamines are controlled drug products frequently used for mild depressions, diet control and certain forms of sleeping ailments. The drugs are in widespread use and generally easily obtainable. The amphetamines function as stimulants, are not thought to be physically addictive and are usually taken orally or by injection. While the amphetamines are responsible for only minor psychological modifications, when taken in combinations with other drugs they may be lethal.

D. Barbiturates

Barbiturates like pentobarbital function as depressants and are used medically for sedation, control of epilepsy and high blood pressure. They are controlled drug products obtainable by prescription and are in relatively widespread use, perhaps less by youth than adults. Barbiturates are taken orally or by injection and are thought to lead to physical dependence.

E. Narcotics

In general narcotics function as depressants and are physically addictive. They are most frequently used in medicine for relief of pain, as anesthetics or for sedation, depending upon the particular narcotic. Most narcotics are taken orally, by injection or sniffed. The following drugs fall in this category.

(1) *Morphine.*
(2) *Heroin.*
(3) *Codeine.*
(4) *Cocaine.* (Not physically addictive.)
(5) *Paregoric.*
(6) *Meperidine.*
(7) *Methadone.*

II. CONTRIBUTING AND CAUSATIVE FACTORS IN DRUG ABUSE

The absence of research on drugs and drug abusers, the emotional climate of parents in facing drug abuse in their children, and the availability and frequency of drug use, make definitive statements on what actually causes a child to turn to drugs difficult if not impossible. At this time, little research can be brought to bear on those factors which cause and those which contribute to a predisposition toward drug abuse. Only hypothetical guesses may be made as tentative explanations for the phenomenon.

A. Type of Drug User

The student who takes drugs does not, by any means, represent a homogenous group with homogenous needs and personality characteristics. The adolescent who experiments with marihuana once or twice is likely to be different from the habitual user.

B. Type of Drug Abuse

While the type of drug used by students in a particular locale depends heavily upon availability and cost, there does appear to be agreement that regular users of marihuana have different dispositions than regular users of hallucinogens or amphetamines or heroin, with the latter probably representing greater personality aberrations than the former. This generalization, however, may not hold with individuals who regularly use drugs, but of different types and at different times.

C. Personality Factors

Drugs may be used as a form of escape, compensation or withdrawal. Individuals with adjustment difficulties, problems with interpersonal relations, anxiety about their futures, etc., may find in drugs and in the drug subculture that form of acceptance which is both rewarding and nonthreatening. Using drugs may facilitate greater feelings of competence and self-esteem and provide, within the subculture, that form of self-concept and identity which offers to resolve those identity crises characteristic of adolescence. While personality factors of a neurotic or pre-neurotic nature may play a role in determining the kind and degree of drug abuse, it is also possible that drug abusers are well-adjusted individuals who purely seek an occasional novelty, excitement and enjoyable high. It is quite likely that no single set of personality characteristics serve to define drug abusers in general.

D. Social Factors

While specific experimental data is lacking, clinical data appears to support that certain social difficulties are somewhat correlated to drug abuse.

(1). *Disturbed family relations.*

Marital conflict, divorce, separation and a break down in communication, respect and dialogue between parents and children may be one contributing social factor to drug abuse or to a failure to appreciate parental cautions and warnings on the problem.

(2). *Disturbed peer relationships.*

The drug subculture provides and satisfies those same kinds of needs as the delinquent-gang structure provided. While leadership and organization of the drug subculture is far less structured and systematic, it does provide a sense of identity, a sharing of secrets and a sense of camaraderie. Individuals who have experienced alienation or isolation from more socially approved group structures as a result of failure in school, poverty, etc., may gravitate to this alternative social organization during school.

E. Political Factors

Youth has increasingly telescoped as a result of technology, communications and television. Students both at the college level and at the secondary level are challenging the relevance and purpose of their institutions. The school has felt the impact of this new awareness more than most institutions. Concern over the Vietnam war, economic and political rights of blacks, students, women and other groups, and, perhaps most importantly, the concern over the relevance of education and the curriculum are some points of confrontation between politicized students and the establishment. The response of these institutions, particularly the school, to these developments has been crucial in either overcoming and resolving differences or reacting so as to increase polarization between parties. The relationship of political movements to drug abuse is not entirely clear, but through polarization, alienation is intensified, the generation gap and credibility gap is enhanced and students are less likely to respond to adult concern over drug abuse. They are less likely to be receptive to drug education programs, which are often viewed as one-sided establishment propaganda, and in some cases, political rebellion may be expressed by a turn toward drugs and drug symbols.

F. Creative Expression

For some, and it would appear a minority of drug users, a desire to expand consciousness, increase inner awareness, examine one's own values, search for new and deeper meanings and more honest and less hypocritical relationships with self and others is an immediate inducement into the drug culture. Many of the symbols in the drug culture point to this characteristic as the primary advantage of the use of drugs. Indeed, many individuals have legitimately taken drugs regularly for these stated purposes.

III. COUNSELING AND DRUG ABUSE

Perhaps the pivot in the entire educational institution which most directly faces the issue of drug abuse is the school counselor. The issue of drug abuse, however, challenges the counseling profession perhaps more than any other issue in recent years. Some elements in the counseling-drug abuse dilemma are worth observing.

A. The Counselor's Objectivity

A number of individuals are still, and perhaps legitimately, shocked by the idea that high school students and junior high school students may be smoking marihuana or habitually taking heroin. In the absence of research a monolithic or stereotyped approach to the drug user may be the counselors initial reaction to his client. His reactions may vary in this instance from a denial of the difficulty of his client, to a stern authoritarian lecture on the evils of drugs, to a violation of the counselor-client relationship and an involvement of the administration, police and courts. In many cases the client may not feel that he has a drug problem but wishes to discuss other concerns. The anxiety of the counselor may make that character of counseling in this example ineffective and impossible. The greatest impediment to effective counseling of the drug user is a failure on the part of the counselor to understand drugs themselves, the particular set of characteristics of his client which predisposes him to drugs and the general amount of objectivity which the counselor can bring to bear on appropriately understanding his client's problems and concerns.

B. Counselor-client confidentiality and counselor responsibility

Perhaps the key issue to effective drug education is the provision in the school for communication to occur. In most states, the counselor does not have the right of privileged communication. In most states, drugs are illegal. A client with a drug problem, therefore, presents a problem which hits the core of counseling itself. If the counselor feels his responsibility rests with the institution and feels an obligation to report instances of drug abuse which come to his attention, the likelihood of his being able to establish *rapport* and *trust* in those students who have drug problems is seriously diminished if nonexistent. If, on the other hand, the counselor attempts to clarify his role and is able to offer a confidential relationship, he must articulate that effectively to the student body, clearly define his role as a person whom a client can trust, and perhaps, face the social, economic and legal compromises such a decision may impose upon him.

C. Counseling resources and techniques

Given that the counselor is in a position to offer confidentiality, his next greatest problem is that of *articulating that confidentiality*. Presentations to individual groups of students or student assemblies on the nature of counseling, the use of anonymous group tapes played for other students to provide a vicarious model drug counseling experience, the use of role playing models, etc., are all vehicles which the counselor has at his disposal to articulate his own function, clarify his image in the school and begin to establish effective individual or group counseling experiences for students with drug problems. Further, the counselor can be a primary agent in *organizing drug education programs,* using group models to discuss and criticize the drug information which is presented. Lastly, the counselor can function as a *referral source* for students having psychotic episodes from drugs. Immediate hospitalization or psychiatric care can be crucial to students on a trip. The need for swift, immediate action is frequently a matter of life and death. Where the counselor is trusted within the drug community, he is likely to be called upon to fulfill this referral function.

CHAPTER **22**

POLITICS, PROTEST AND AUTHORITY

INTRODUCTION. Within the last few years our educational system, particularly at the university level, has acted as a melting pot for new values, philosophies and political ideologies. Few, if any, universities have been spared the experience of demonstrations, picketing, strikes and the more violent forms of militancy. The polarization and radicalization of these new student movements has proceeded rapidly. More recently the wave of student action has reached the secondary school. While in many respects the volume of student activities which can be characterized as protest still is larger at the university level, an increasing number of protests have occurred in the high schools and junior high schools, and the trend appears to show that they will grow. It is the purpose of this chapter to analyze the issues nested in these controversies and to examine the role of counseling and guidance with respect to them.

I. THE ISSUES

Issues are rarely identical from school to school. Neither are the students who support them. The literature, however, provides some general perception of emerging trends in the school body politic.

A. Curriculum relevancy

Schools have a way of institutionalizing the curriculum. If a course is offered once, it is likely to be offered again, carried by its own inertia. If the subject continues for a longer period of time, it begins to represent a "skill" which everyone must have. While schools do conduct evaluations of curricula and do attempt to modernize subjects, a large number of students at the secondary level feel constricted by the curriculum, fail to appreciate its short or long term relevancy and tend to be alienated from the educational system by their response to the subjects offered. Furthermore, the immediacy of certain social issues like the Vietnam war, racial strife and the need of certain social or racial groups to have courses dealing with their own needs and backgrounds, e.g. black studies, make an inflexible and un-inspired curriculum the object of attack and protest. Not only does a protest over curricular relevance make educators face the dilemma of evaluating, changing and revising the curriculum, but it raises a sometimes more heated issue of student curricular planning, i.e. giving students a voice in the selection and deter-mination of the curriculum.

B. Rules, Obedience and Authority

A second major focus of conflict is on the nature of authority and the role of respect and obedience. Students today appear to find a relativity in rules of conduct more than they may have some years ago. Experience with civil obedience growing out of the integration movements and the publicized controversies over the war tend to give students the belief that some rules are wrong or inappropriate, and it is one's right, if not duty, to change them. A school which has an inflexible policy with regard to rules of conduct, dress, etc., and which does not have the machinery to democratically address these rules and to change them through student government channels, is likely to feel the impact of student discontent and rebellion.

C. Function of rules

Closely related to the apparent decreasing respect for author-ity is the increasing student examination of rules themselves. Are rules made for efficient organization and administration of the curriculum, for example, or are they merely there as a con-venience for the management and control of student behavior? Do rules governing dress have any relevance to education, and if so, what is the relationship, or do rules of dress and conduct merely reflect the whims of a conservative administration? How are these seemingly irrelevant rules made? Who is consulted in making and determining these policies? These are some of the questions which students are asking. The short term solution appears to be to discontinue or modify those rules which come under student disfavor. The long term problem and solution is more dramatic. Will students be given more liberties by their own hand, will they have control, or will they be appeased with the control and decision-making power still resting in the hands of the administration?

D. Civil rights for students

Students are taught from early elementary school onward that they live in a democracy and that each citizen is free to choose or say what he believes. At the same time a student in high school realizes the he has few, if any, legal rights, and that he, like other minority groups, is discriminated against in inumerable ways. It may be argued that full rights of citizenship come at a certain age and that these rights require certain responsibilities, but the pendulum appears to swing in the other direction with students wanting more rights, more dignity and more access to the machinery for change earlier than the "establishment" might be willing to surrender it.

E. Militancy vs. democracy

It is not difficult to find a school with certain pressing issues which expresses student opinion legitimately and democratically through its student government apparatus and through its elected student representatives. It is not difficult either to find in such a school a long history of administration veto of student proposed changes. On the other hand, it is not difficult to find a school in which students have not even explored the possibilities of democratic change through the student government machinery, but have instead planned disruptive and violent encounters to dramatize the urgency and necessity for change, even with a sensitive administration which is more likely to respect student demands if they are expressed through appropriate channels. What appears is that students have learned that the administration and the adult community respond more quickly and attentively to a riot or strike than they do a polite request. There is a growing disenchantment with the democratic process as a means for change. Militancy, it would appear, will be the means of change and of protest as long as it is rewarded for its efforts.

II. ROLE OF THE COUNSELOR

The counselor is not the remedy for resolving many of these issues. Moreover, the role of the counselor might easily be disputed among counseling professionals as to how he should behave in these kinds of crises. Some sketches, however, may be made which express and define some possible roles counselors might adopt.

A. Counselor as ombudsman

Schools, whose machinery for communication and dialogue has broken down, may resort to the use of an outside mediator or ombudsmanlike party. In this role, the counselor-ombudsman serves both the students and administration by appropriately articulating each side's point of view to the other clearly and objectively. While there are few, if any, references to the counselor acting in this way, there does not appear to be any intrinsic conflict in such a role. In this capacity, the counselor is similar to a labor-mediator and, if effective, can warrant respect and trust from both sides.

B. Counselor as research specialist on student opinion

The counselor is trained to construct tests and to evaluate them statistically. In many ways a student protest represents a failure of the counseling staff to know the concerns and needs of the students they wish to serve. It is within the counseling function to assess, survey and poll student opinion and from those results make recommendations to the administration on needed changes.

C. Counselor as specialist in interpersonal communications

Frequently, conflict has occurred in schools between students, groups of students and races. In these cases a counselor might wish to attempt to structure sensitivity and other group experiences which allow students an opportunity to understand how each other feels, and perceives the dilemma etc. Activities of this sort which emphasize many of the new techniques of group process and group dynamics are still quite sparse in frequency. Such a model, however, for these kinds of group conflicts would appear much more suited to the problem than those kinds of educational activities which might characterize a more traditional group guidance course.

III. PROBLEMS FOR THE COUNSELOR

Certain difficulties emerge when considering the counselor in the school with political and social problems.

A. Confidentiality

Is the counselor to serve as an informer, to provide the administration with the names of students who plan disruptive actions, or is he to respect his confidences even when he knows he might be able to prevent violence or other disorders?

B. Articulation and role-perception

Will the counselor be able to articulate his role to both students and to the administration that he can effectively operate for the mutual benefit of both sides in the controversy, or will he be seen by students as ineffective, irrelevant or untrustworthy?

CHAPTER 23

CONTINUING SOCIAL CRISES

INTRODUCTION. The previous chapters devoted to under-achievement, drug abuse and political activities treat relatively discrete and current social issues which may be new to the counselor leaving his graduate training program and entering his first professional school assignment. Some other social problems, however, have plagued counseling for a somewhat longer period of time, which is not to say that counselors are any closer to techniques and solutions for dealing with these problems. The problems of *delinquency, school dropouts, illegitimacy* and *venereal disease* are the continuing social crises of our time and will probably be so for quite some time. It is the purpose of this chapter to review some of the basic features of these problems and discuss the relationship of the counselor to each. As with other social problems, the school can only act in a partial way in either contributing to the problem or in serving to remedy it inasmuch as other factors like economic, family and cultural factors exert influences upon children which play a contributing role in their appearance. The role of the counselor, therefore, has imposed upon it some limits on the degree to which it can change all of these determinants which effect a given child and make any kind of total positive change.

I. THE SCHOOL DROPOUT

A student who leaves school before receiving his high school education increasingly constitutes a social problem, for the probabilities are strongly in favor of his greater reliance upon public assistance and welfare, his severe job limitations and unemployment and for his greater participation in crime and violence than for any other social group to which he can be compared. As society expands its technology, the probability that school

234

dropouts will find suitable places in it further decreases. About *30 percent* of school age children and young adults do not receive a high school diploma. While fewer drop out each year, and this progress is marked over previous generations, the problems which this group is to face erases the positive gains which might otherwise be comfortable to stress.

A. Reasons for dropping out

Most studies point to the following reasons students do not complete high school:

1. *Desire to work and earn money.*
2. *Desire to get married.*
3. *School failure.*
4. *Courses in school are irrelevant.*
5. *Poor relationships with teachers and peers.*

B. Characteristics of dropouts

While data gathering on dropouts tends to be related to the area sampled, some general comparisons may be drawn (Leubling, 1967).

1. *Approximately half of the dropouts have average or better intelligence.*
2. *About 25 percent have delinquency records.*
3. *A majority have never failed a grade in high school.*
4. *Approximately half have never had a conference with a counselor.*
5. *About 70 percent had parents who were neither separated nor divorced.*
6. *Half of the dropouts have fathers whose work is either unskilled or semi-skilled.*

C. Counseling and the school dropout

The general figures above do not complete a description of any one child, but instead provide a mosaic in which dropouts may be found. Poverty, failure, broken homes, intelligence and many other variables affect some students in the direction of dropping out of school. No single variable appears to account for the problem. As such, the counselor must approach dropout prevention from an individual point of view. His skills and training can offer the school some needed resources in addressing the problem.

1. *Identification of potential school dropouts.*
2. *Helping to establish dropout prevention programs.*
3. *Use of group counseling processes with potential dropouts.*
4. *Providing meaningful occupational and educational information researches and experiences.*
5. *Individual counseling.*

II.   DELINQUENCY

On the average the increase in juvenile crime and delinquency as measured by the number of cases handled by juvenile courts is estimated to be increasing by two to three times the increase in population of this age group. This alarming increase reflects increasing sensitivity and attention to the problem by the police and courts, but also reflects a real increase as well. Like other social problems, delinquency is not a discrete, isolated issue but instead, is interwoven with other precipitating factors such as poverty, the family, social and neighborhood factors and educational variables (Graubard, 1969).

A.   Delinquency offences

Boys tend to pose a greater problem in this area than girls. Of the more significant offenses coming under the attention of the juvenile courts, the following offenses are most common.

1. *Vandalism.*
2. *Auto theft.*
3. *Truancy, runaway and curfew violations.*
4. *Robbery and burglary.*
5. *Larceny.*

B.   Causes of delinquency

Some general etiological factors may be given for the phenomenon of juvenile crime.

1. *Disparity between economic and social aspirations versus opportunity.*
2. *Discrimination and slow access to educational and economic opportunity.*
3. *Family disorganization.*
4. *Alienation and acculturated anti-social behavior adaptations.*

C. Delinquency and education

There are a surprising number of relationships between educational variables and delinquency.

1. *Over half of the delinquents have failed one or more grades and are average for their grade.*
2. *Over 90 percent of the delinquent offenders have had problems of truancy and misconduct in school.*
3. *Over 80 percent of delinquent offenders are school dropouts.*

D. The counselor's role

Delinquency is one problem counselors have had little success with over the years. The problem as it appears at the school level is invariably symptomatic of deeper difficulties rooted elsewhere: in the home, the ghetto environment, etc. In many respects the school is the meeting ground of middle class values and expectations face to face with lower class and slum realities. For the majority of delinquent youth, a weekly individual counseling experience is a very inadequate therapeutic measure. While group procedures may have some value in the treatment of *certain* individual delinquents or pre-delinquents, the greatest points of emphasis for the counselor appear to lie in the following areas:

1. *Acting with other school professionals to restructure the school and curriculum to achieve relevancy with the local environmental realities.*
2. *Emphasis upon vocational and employment factors in the guidance program.*
3. *Acting as a liaison with community agencies, e.g. youth mobilization centers, half-way houses, the courts, etc.*

III. ILLEGITIMACY AND VENEREAL DISEASE

The rapid social and cultural changes occurring in America have given rise to new values and attitudes regarding sexual expression. For the middle class, at least, this has meant greater sexual freedom, earlier sexual contact and a higher incidence in this group of venereal disease and illegitimacy. For lower class youth, these social and cultural changes have had less of an impact in terms of being responsible for new sexual expression; the more immediate factors of poverty, poor housing, family disorganization, etc., have contributed to the traditionally high level of promiscuity, illegitimacy and venereal disease in this group.

A. The problem

Both venereal disease and illegitimate births are on an alarming increase. Since 1950, the number of children born illegitimate has increased almost *three times* (population increases held constant). Similarly, in the last six years gonorrhea has increased over 35 percent in the United States and constitutes a public health menace that has reached epidemic proportion. In this same period, however, infectious syphilis has decreased as a result of better treatment and a current public health campaign. Most cases of venereal disease are reported by the poor and the young.

B. The counselor's role

In addressing himself to the problem the counselor must be aware of his local situation and the kind of clients with whom he deals. He must be aware of the implications of a series of new developments occurring in the area of sex education, sex technology and sex law. State boards of education are rapidly outlining programs in sex education. New laws are being passed regarding legalized abortion. New policies are being established both in welfare agencies and other community agencies with regard to the provision of birth control information. Universities are struggling with the question of providing birth control devices to unmarried women. Apart from the traditional counseling process related to these questions, the counselor must address himself to these new social, legal and political questions and be able to act upon the most current information and status of these various questions. Some of the characteristics of the counselor's role may be outlined below:

1. *Individual and group pre-marital counseling.*
2. *Sponsorship of sex education and birth control information activities with other school professionals.*
3. *Service as a consultant to the sex education program.*
4. *Sponsorship with other school professionals of venereal disease control programs.*
5. *Acting as a resource and referral source with outside persons and agencies.*

CHAPTER **24**

CONTROVERSIES IN COUNSELING AND GUIDANCE

INTRODUCTION. Counseling and guidance is replete with controversy. The multitude of issues around which one may take a contrary position is vast and attests, in a fundamental way, to the growth and health of the entire movement in America. A survey of some basic controversies in counseling and guidance and the arguments for each position is the purpose of this chapter (Schertzer & Stone, 1966).

I. IS GUIDANCE TO BE DISTINGUISHED FROM TEACHING?

A. Yes

The teacher's responsibility concerns the transmission of knowledge and skills. The teacher must maintain an evaluative attitude in assessing and rewarding student progress. Such an orientation toward subject matter rather than the child, and toward evaluation rather than understanding and rapport, are incompatible with the nonevaluative, personal orientation of the counselor. For these reasons teaching and guidance are distinct school functions.

B. No

The child cannot be subdivided into specialties where counselors deal with emotional concerns, teachers deal with academic and instructional matters and administrators with other aspects of the youngster. Good education is education of the whole child. An approach which is not integrated and focused upon the whole child is an invalid one. For this reason teaching and guidance must be considered together.

II. MUST CERTIFIED SCHOOL COUNSELORS HAVE TEACHING EXPERIENCE?

A. Yes

Teaching and counseling are mutually related school functions requiring mutual understanding. A counselor must have teaching experience to understand the major function of the school. Without teaching experience the counselor would be an outsider, and individuals from many disciplines would occupy positions as counselors solely because this would be the only avenue open to them to enter the educational scene without certification and teacher preparation.

B. No

The need for counselors is great, and requiring counselors to come from the ranks of teachers keeps the source of supply small. Counseling is a distinct discipline from teaching requiring specialized training in the social sciences. Highly qualified persons in these disciplines are currently being denied access to counseling roles in our schools because of the discriminatory nature of the teaching experience certification prerequisites.

III. SHOULD THE USE OF THE WORD "GUIDANCE" BE ELIMINATED?

A. Yes

Not only is guidance an ambiguous term, but it connotes an approach to the child which implies discipline, directiveness and general authoritarianism; a point of view held only by a very small minority of professional guidance specialists.

B. No

Guidance as a term has historical roots and has come to signify an entire school function which is neither administrative nor instructional. Substituting a more modern term would detract from its historical strength.

IV. SHOULD THE ADMINISTRATION AND PUBLIC DETERMINE THE COUNSELOR'S ROLE AND DUTIES?

A. Yes

The counselor exists to serve the needs of a particular school having particular and unique characteristics. The persons best qualified to know these needs are the hiring public and the local school administration.

B. No

The counselor is a specialist with unique skills and competencies. As a professional, he has the right to use his own judgment concerning how and where those competencies will be implemented.

V. IS THE SCHOOL COUNSELOR A PSYCHOLOGIST?

A. Yes

While the counselor exists in the schools, so too do social workers, psychologists and psychiatrists. The counseling function is essentially a psychological function. Counseling is a form of psychotherapy dealing with normal individuals. As such the counselor is more psychologist or behavioral scientist than an educator.

B. No

The counselor exists in an educational setting and his training includes, but is not *limited to, psychology.* In fact, most counselors are trained in schools and colleges of education. He is not a therapist but an educational facilitator in the schools. Therefore, he is an educator not a psychologist.

VI. SHOULD THE COUNSELOR BE INVOLVED WITH SCHOOL DISCIPLINE?

A. Yes

A discipline problem is basically a psychological one requiring specialized attention by a professional schooled in human behavior and its causes. Not assuming responsibility for discipline leaves the counselor with a passive and conforming population of counselees not those truly in need of help.

B. No

Discipline is a process of enforcing school rules and involves forcing conformity. To assume responsibility for disciplinary cases, the counselor takes on an authoritarian role and loses the accepting and nonevaluative role perception essential for self-referrals and meaningful counseling.

VII. SHOULD SCHOOL COUNSELORS DEAL ONLY WITH EDUCATIONAL-VOCATIONAL COUNSELING?

A. Yes

The historical and public expectation and image of counselors is that they assist youth with educational and career problems. Moreover, the counselor is less well trained to engage in personal–social counseling than the psychologist. He should stay in his own area of competency: educational and vocational guidance.

B. No

The counselor is trained to assist students with whatever concerns them. Moreover, the child requiring vocational assistance frequently has concerns of a personal nature. The former cannot be effectively understood in the absence of the latter. Counseling must focus on the whole spectrum of student concerns. Furthermore, a school counselor trained at the masters' level often has more practicum experience in personal–social individual counseling than his school psychological counterpart.

VIII. SHOULD COUNSELORS USE TESTS IN COUNSELING?

A. Yes

The use of tests gives the counselor a reliable means of observing behavior which he might not otherwise see. Tests enable the counselor to make a diagnosis and to understand the child better, thereby facilitating counseling and referral. Tests may also be used to help the child express feelings and ventilate attitudes which he might not feel free to do in a less structured setting. The interpretation of test behavior can be a therapeutic experience for the child.

B. No

Counseling is essentially a personal relationship between a counselor and a client. The imposition of impersonal and mechanistic devices such as tests into such a personal relationship is incompatible and harmful. Testing places the counselor in the role of an expert who uses test data to tell the client what is wrong with him. Testing makes the counseling relationship impersonal and paternalistic.

COMMENTARY. There is no way to exhaustively cover all of the livelier issues in counseling and guidance. Instead, the issues above represent those issues most often treated in the literature of counseling and guidance. However, the literature often lags behind the contemporary scene. Some other issues might be whether counselors should deal with drug abuse; whether they should deal with severely disturbed clients with psychiatric histories (when there are no agencies to deal with these clients); whether a counselor should give clients advice, or suggestions; whether a counselor has complete confidentiality and privileged communication with his clients; whether a school counselor should do staff sensitivity training or group work with teachers and administrators; whether a counselor should affiliate himself with a professional teacher union; whether the counselor should have a role in drug education and sex education programs which may be incorporated in the curriculum; whether the counselor has a *vested* interest in teachers performing counseling functions; especially sensitivity activities in their classrooms, etc. These issues are perhaps less often treated, but still represent some of the more vital controversies in counseling psychology and guidance.

BIBLIOGRAPHY

Alexander, F.M. & French, T.M.: *Psychoanalytic Therapy*. New York, The Ronald Press Co., 1946.

American Psychiatric Association: *Diagnostic and Statistical Manual, Mental Disorders*. Washington, D.C., Author, 1952.

Anastasi, A.: *Psychological Testing*. London, Macmillan and Co., Ltd., 1968.

Ansbacher, H. & Ansbacher, R.: *The Individual Psychology of Alfred Adler*. New York, Basic Books, 1956.

Blocher, D.H.: *Developmental Counseling*. New York, The Ronald Press Co., 1966.

Bordin, E.S.: *Psychological Counseling*. New York, Appleton-Century-Crofts, 1955.

Borow, H.: *Man in a World of Work*. Boston, Houghton Mifflin Co., 1964

Brammer, L.M. & Shostrom, E.L.: *Therapeutic Psychology*. Englewood Cliffs, Prentice-Hall, Inc., 1968.

Brenner, C.: *An Elementary Textbook of Psychoanalysis*. New York, Doubleday Anchor Books, 1955.

Coleman, J.C.: *Abnormal Psychology and Modern Life*, 3rd. ed. Glenview, Scott, Foresman and Company, 1964.

Cottingham, H.F.: Guidance in the elementary school—a status review. In D.C., Dinkmeyer: *Guidance and Counseling in the Elementary School*. New York, Holt, Rinehart and Winston, Inc., 1968.

Erikson, E.H.: *Childhood and Society*. New York, W.W. Norton and Company, Inc., 1950.

Frankl, V.E.: *Man's Search for Meaning*. Boston, Beacon Press, 1962.

Glanz, E.C.: *Foundations and Principles of Guidance*. Boston, Allyn and Bacon, Inc., 1964.

Ginzberg, E., Ginsburg, S.W., Axelrad, S. & Herma, J.L.: *Occupational Choice: An Approach to a General Theory*. New York, Columbia University Press, 1951.

Graubard, P. (Ed.): *Children Against Schools*. Chicago, Follett Educational Corporation, 1969.

Grinker, R.R.: A transactional model for psychotherapy. In M.I., Stein (Ed.): *Contemporary Psychotherapies*. New York, Free Press, 1961.

Hall, J.F.: *The Psychology of Learning*. New York, J.B. Lippincott Co., 1966.

Holland, J.L.: A theory of vocational choice. *Journal of Counseling Psychology, 6* (No. 1): 35–44; 1959.

Hollis, J.W. & Hollis, L.U.: *Personalizing Information Processes*. London, Macmillan and Co., Ltd., 1969.

Hutt, M.L. & Gibby, R.G.: *The Mentally Retarded Child* 2nd ed. Boston, Allyn and Bacon, Inc., 1965.

Kroth, J.A.: *A Programmed Primer in Learning Disabilities.* Springfield, Charles C Thomas, Pub. 1971.

Leubling, H.: Counseling with dropouts: a three-year study. *Vocational Guidance Quarterly, 15*:173–180; 1967.

Norris, W., Zeran, F.R. & Hatch, R.N.: *The Information Service in Guidance.* Chicago, Rand McNally & Co., 1966.

Peters, H.J. & Farwell, G.F.: *Guidance: A Developmental Approach.* Chicago, Rand McNally & Co., 1967.

Roe, A.: Early determinants of vocational choice. *Journal of Counseling Psychology, 4* (No. 3): 212–217; 1957.

Rogers, C.R.: A theory of therapy, personality and interpersonal relationships as developed in the client-centered framework. In S., Kock (Ed.): *Psychology: A Study of Science.* New York, McGraw-Hill, Inc., 1959.

Salter, A.: *Conditioned Reflex Therapy.* New York, Capricorn, 1961.

Schertzer, B. & Stone, S.: *Fundamentals of Guidance.* Boston, Houghton Mifflin Co., 1966.

Schertzer, B. & Stone, S.: *Fundamentals of Counseling.* Boston, Houghton Mifflin Co., 1968.

Schmidt, L.D.: Some legal considerations for counseling and clinical psychologists. *Journal of Counseling Psychology, 9*:35–44; 1962.

Schutz, W.C.: *Joy.* New York, Grove Press, Inc., 1967.

Super, D.E.: A theory of vocational development. *Am Psychol, 8* (No. 4): 185–190; 1953.

Terman, L.M. & Merrill, M.A.: *Measuring Intelligence.* Boston, Houghton Mifflin Co., 1937.

Tiedeman, D.V.: Decision and vocational development: a paradigm and its implications. *Personnel and Guidance Journal, 40*:15–20; 1961.

Thorne, F.C.: Personality: a clinical eclectic viewpoint. *J Clin Psychol,* 1961.

Wechsler D.: *Manual for the Wechsler Adult Intelligence Scale.* New York, Psychological Corporation, 1955.

Wechsler, D.: *The Measurement and Appraisal of Adult Intelligence.* Baltimore, The Williams & Wilkins Co., 1958.

Wolman, B.B.: *Contemporary Theories and Systems in Psychology.* New York, Harper & Bros., 1960.

Wolpe, J. & Lazarus, A.A.: *Behavior Therapy Techniques.* New York, Pergamon Press Inc., 1966.

INDEX

A

Abreaction, 129
A-B-C theory of personality, 125
Acute brain disorders, 21
Adler A., 35
Alcoholism, 20
Alexander, F., 132
American Personnel and Guidance
Association, 67
American Psychological
Association, 67
Amnesia, 11
Anorexia nervosa, 13
Auditory perceptual deficits, 219
Avoidance conditioning, 45

B

Behavior therapy, 127–128, 154
Bordin, E., 130

C

Case study, 191
Chronic brain disorders, 21
Classical conditioning, 43
Combat exhaustion, 7
Conditioned reflex therapy, 127
Conversion reaction, 8
Conant, J., 65
Counseling
    certification, 113
    counselor role, 116, 220, 227, 233
    counselor-student ratios, 113
    definition of, 120
    preparation, 115–116
    stages of, 147–148
    supply and demand, 113
    techniques, 141–145
    versus psychotherapy, 121
Countertransference, 148
Cretinism, 216

Cultural-familial retardation, 217
Cyclothymic personality, 18

D

Delinquency, 236–237
Denial, 30
Desensitization, 129–130
Diagnosis, 146–147
Disaster syndrome, 9
Dissociative reaction, 11

E

Ego, 29
Eigenwelt, 137
Elementary guidance, 205–211
Ellis, A., 125–126
Enuresis, 17
Erikson, E., 37–39
Eros, 25–26
Ethics in counseling, 117–120
Expert witness, 117–118
Extinction, 47

F

Free association, 133
Frankl, V., 138
Frequency distribution, 181
Freud, S., 24–31
Fugue, 11

G

Ginzberg, E., 197
Grinker, R., 137
Group behavior modification, 154
Group dynamics, 151
Guidance
    and administration, 80
    and curriculum, 79–80
    and teachers, 78
    definition, 55

247

history, 60–65
need for, 56
philosophy of, 70–72
specialists, 85–88
Guthrie, E., 48

H

Halo effect, 185
Hallucinogens, 222
Holland, J., 201
Hull, C., 50
Hydrocephaly, 216
Hypertension, 12
Hysteria, 10

I

Id, 29
Intelligence tests, 169–172, 217
Involutional psychotic reaction, 16
Irreversibility of occupational
  choice, 197

J

Jung, C., 31–34

K

Koffka, K., 49
Kohler, W., 49
Kuder Preference Record, 175

L

La belle indifference, 10
Leads, 143–145

M

Manic depressive reaction, 15
Marathon groups, 154
Marihuana, 222
Mean, 182
Median, 182
Migraines, 12
Mitwelt, 137
Mode, 182
Mongolism, 216
Multiple personality, 11

N

Need hierarchy, 198
Neurasthenia, 10
Normalcy, 5–7
Normal curve, 182

O

Obesity, 12
Observations, 186
Obsessive compulsive reaction, 10
Oedipus complex, 27
O'Hara, R., 202–203
Operant conditioning, 45

P

Paranoia, 14
Parsons, F., 65
Passive aggressive personality, 18
Percentile, 184
Persona, 33
Peptic ulcers, 12
Phobias, 11
Placement service, 104
Play therapy, 208
Process limits, 142
Process theory of psychotherapy,
  135–136
Projective techniques, 176
Psychic determinism, 25
Psychodrama, 153
Psychoneurosis, 9–11
Psychopath, 19
Psychosomatic disorders, 11–13

R

Random sample, 184
Reaction formation, 30
Reciprocal inhibition, 128
Reflection, 144
Regression, 29
Reliability, 167
Repression, 29
Research and evaluation, 106–109
Resistance, 148
Roe, A., 198–199
Rogers, C., 39–41, 134–136
Role playing, 144

S

Salter, A., 127
Schedules of reinforcement, 46
Schizophrenia, 13–14
School dropouts, 234
Shadow, 33
Silence, 144
Slander and libel, 118
Social learning, 48
Sociogram, 190
Sociopathic personality, 19
Somnambulism, 11
Spontaneous recovery, 47
Standard deviation, 183
Stanine, 184
Stimulus generalization, 47
Strong, E., 174
Structuring, 142–143
Stuttering, 17
Super, D., 199–200
Superego, 30

T

T-groups, 153
Thanatos, 26
Thorne, F., 124

Tics, 17
Tiedeman, D., 202–203
Tolman, C., 49–50
Trait-factor counseling approach, 123–127
Transference, 133, 148
Transparency, 141

U

Umwelt, 137
Undoing, 30

V

Validity, 168
Venereal disease, 238
Visual perceptual deficits, 219

W

Wechsler Intelligence Scale for Children (WISC), 172–173
Wertheimer, M., 49
Williamson, E., 123
Wolpe, J., 127
Wrenn, C., 65

Z

Z scores, 184